One
Heart
Rejoicing

To order additional copies of *One Heart Rejoicing,*
by Don C. Schneider, call 1-800-765-6955.
Visit us at www.reviewandherald.com for information on
other Review and Herald products.

DON C. SCHNEIDER

The Difference
Jesus Makes
One
Heart
Rejoicing

REVIEW AND HERALD® PUBLISHING ASSOCIATION
HAGERSTOWN, MD 21740

The author assumes full responsibility for the accuracy of all facts and quotations as cited in this book.

This book was
Edited by Ron Knott
Copyedited by Jocelyn Fay and Lori Halvorsen
Designed by Tina M. Ivany
Cover art by Joel D. Springer
Electronic makeup by Tina M. Ivany
Typeset: 11/14 Bembo

PRINTED IN U.S.A.

05 04 03 02 01   5   4   3   2   1

R&H Cataloging Service
Schneider, Don C. 1942-
    One heart rejoicing: the difference Jesus makes.

    1. Christian life.   I. Title

                    248.4

ISBN 0-8280-1602-X

In memory of my parents,

V. O. and Myrtle Schneider

Mom said, "Don't talk discouragement; go out and make a difference."

Dad said, "Jesus has done so much for my family; you must do everything you can for Him."

Acknowledgments

These editorials were written to appear in the *Lake Union Herald* while I was president of the Lake Union from 1994 through 2000. You will see, occasionally, in the writing the things that were happening in my own life. My mother and father both died during those six years, as did my wife's mother. You will see some editorials that speak of grieving and of comfort. Our son went to medical school and did an internship in New Guinea, and he now wants to go back to New Guinea as a missionary doctor as soon as his residency is over. Our daughter graduated from college and became a teacher in Adventist schools. You will see some editorials that show our pride, because there is no higher calling than to be part of the work of God's church. Because of these events happening in our lives and around these editorials, you occasionally will find notes at the end of the editorials indicating when it was printed and what additional events may have transpired since.

Sometimes the editorials appeared as if inspiration virtually dictated them to me. More often they were dragged—almost kicking and literally screaming (at least some people tell me there was screaming)—from my brain and from my computer. Once in a while the editorial idea had to be stuffed back into my brain in order to have a little more work done on it.

If the editorials have value it is because Jesus truly is my friend. But many other people helped the editorials become literate works of writing. My wife, Marti, would take my ideas and help them become paragraphs. The capable staff of the *Lake Union Herald*—Dick Dower, Nadine Dower, and Ann

Fisher—struggled with my often contorted syntax and put in commas and took out commas in order to make the piece more readable. (They also taught me a new word: syntax. I had thought it was a fee the government levied on illegal activity!)

This book project wouldn't have come into being without Dick Dower. He thought of the idea, played with it, shaped it, then encouraged me to feel that readers would find value in seeing the editorials again. Finally, he handed the project to Mark Thomas and Jeannette Johnson at the Review and Herald Publishing Association.

And then there was Kermit Netteburg, assistant to the North American Division president for communication. He is the one who actually ran the book project and took care of the details in making it happen.

Jesus is my friend; I hope He is your friend, too. If you are not sure that He is your friend, please start the friendship as you read this book.

—Don C. Schneider
December 2000

Contents

Jesus Is My Friend

Jesus is my friend. We became friends one Friday night as I knelt beside my bed in my dormitory room at Wisconsin Academy. Of course, I had known about Him before. In fact, I could pass all the Bible tests, argue religion with people, offer public prayers, or even give public lip service to His name. But knowing *about* Jesus is not the same as *knowing* Him. Knowing about Jesus does not necessarily make one happy, but knowing Jesus as a personal friend and Saviour will.

Our family was introduced to Jesus in northern Wisconsin by a dedicated church elder who answered the Bible questions we asked, and then proceeded to give us Bible studies that eventually led to baptism. Within a few months I was enrolled in the Merrill, Wisconsin, church school, where my teacher helped me to grow in Jesus. But later, when I was a teenager, I lost sight of Him. However, on a special Friday night at Wisconsin Academy, Jesus became my friend once again.

Having an experience with Jesus, you see, is not just a once-in-a-lifetime thing, nor even a once-a-year thing. Just a few years ago I visited Wisconsin Academy. I went to the boys' dorm, found the assistant dean, and asked to see my old room. There the assistant dean joined me as I knelt by the bed again and rededicated my life to Jesus. I want my experience with Jesus to be a constant one. And I would like the same for you. As I write this I'm inviting Jesus in again right now. And as you read this I invite you to give yourself to Jesus too. In fact, I invite you to commit the rest of your life to Him.

They Are Worthless!

The pastor said it. Probably I would have agreed with him if I had been riding in his car that night. He and his head elder had just been to the home of a family to invite them to consider baptism. The man of the house had often been away at the bar on the days he had committed to study the Bible with the elder. The wife didn't seem to be ready to make a decision for Jesus either.

So could I blame the pastor for his evaluation of the family? They didn't look like prospects for the church at all. From his viewpoint, as far as their being interests for the church, they were worthless. He advised the elder not to bother with them anymore. *No use investing time in people who seem to show so little interest in spiritual things.*

It is right, I suppose, to classify your interests. It is good policy to spend your time where it will count. Why just keep on with people who don't seem to be responding?

I wondered that about Elmer Trinen. One pastor after another had talked to him about committing himself to Jesus, but he didn't seem interested. But when we moved to town his wife wanted me to talk with him too. I was a brand-new pastor and didn't know much about classifying interests. I just kept going to see him, kept on being his friend. We kept praying for him . . . and one day *he* told *me* he wanted to be baptized.

Paul didn't look like a good interest either. He spent his time harassing Christians. Who would ever have thought that he could become an evangelist? But Jesus didn't give up on him. The members, on the other hand, were so afraid of him that they wouldn't accept him even though he told them that he had changed. They had a real "wait and see" attitude.

Have you thought about giving up on praying for someone? . . . for a sister? . . . a brother? . . . a neighbor? . . . for your kids? Don't do it! They may look like "worthless interests" to someone else, but don't give up. *Evangelism,* page 626, says that none have fallen too low, and *Education,* page 29, says that a desire to do good is in every person.

That head elder heard the pastor's evaluation of the Bible study interests, but he just couldn't give up on the family. He kept coming back. In fact, even though it looked as if it might do no good at all, for a second time he started right at the beginning of the Bible study series and went through all 28 lessons again. That's when *our* family started going to church. I'm glad the elder didn't accept the evaluation. I'm glad that he kept coming to see us. We may have looked worthless to some people, but not to the elder, and not to Jesus, either.

There are none who are worthless. Never stop praying for them. Never give up. Jesus is still working on their hearts.

I Did a Good Deed

As far as good deeds go, this ranks right up there as one of the best. I almost messed it up, though. It does not come easy for me, but I'm trying to do this kind of good deed often. And I have asked God to help me. Without Him, I know there is no way I can do it.

This good deed was a real winner. A man is a better man because of it. Without my good deed he could have been wounded. In fact, his whole family could have been hurt. Sounds heroic, doesn't it? Like saving them from a burning building? Actually he wasn't present at the time, so he doesn't know about my good deed. In fact, he may never know about it. I don't plan to tell him. And those around me at the time don't know about it, nor do I plan to tell them. That would destroy the whole thing.

I'm not going to tell *you* all about it either. There won't be a feature story with pictures. I'll tell you just enough so that you can see what kind of good deed it was, but you'll not learn the name of the person or the actual good deed.

Here it is: I knew something bad that I didn't tell.

That's it. Simple, huh? Do you *really* think so? It certainly would have been easier for me to talk. Yes, I knew something bad about the man. What I knew was true, too! The others in the group didn't know anything about it. Can you imagine how much fun it would have been to break the story? But they didn't need to know. It would only have made the man look bad. In fact, it would really have detracted from his reputation and might have ruined his career. *My good deed was that I knew something bad, and I didn't tell it.*

How many times does this same good deed need to be done around our churches? There are plenty of true things that we know that do not *need* to be told. Keeping quiet doesn't come naturally for most of us. The grandmother of a friend of mine wrote in the flyleaf of her Bible a standard by which to judge what she would say. "Is it kind? Is it true? Is it necessary?" It is so easy to say unkind, unnecessary things about one another. In fact, I cannot keep myself from doing it on my own, so I have asked Jesus to help me. I pray King David's prayer (Psalm 141:3): "Set a watch, O Lord, before my mouth; keep the door of my lips." With Jesus empowering us to overcome this enticing temptation, our churches, schools, and communities will be more positive and joyful. They'll be places where we respect and value one another in Christian love.

All together, every day, let's pray: "Set a watch, O Lord, before my mouth; keep the door of my lips."

I'm Obsessed

The airline ticket agent was wrong. She had no right to treat me like that. When I asked about using an old unused ticket on a flight, she told me that the useful date had now expired. But along with that explanation came a lot of questions about where I was on a certain day a month ago, how I had flown to Los Angeles the evening before (that was my son, Don) and gotten back already to make *this* flight . . . and a lot of questions that seemed to be actually inappropriate. Mostly it was her attitude. I could hardly believe that it was happening. She was acting like a prosecuting attorney, and I seemed to be guilty of some crime.

When I left the counter to get on the airplane, I was distressed. No, that is not the right word. I was irritated. No, I was angry and obsessed. For the next several hours I thought about it almost constantly. I went over and over the letter that I wanted to send to her supervisor and thought about who should be sent copies of it.

After several hours, a night's sleep, and some time with my Bible, it dawned on me how senseless it was to allow this incident to become such an obsession with me. Thinking about it constantly was not making me more like Jesus. It was not making me a kinder person. And reviewing the episode certainly didn't make me feel better. I was not enjoying life more because of this obsession.

The subject of my Bible reading that day was about the sanctuary in the wilderness. As I came to the section about the mercy seat, it struck me that I want to be obsessed, all right—obsessed with being like Jesus. I want to spend time reading about Him. I want to spend time just thinking about Him. I want to spend time talking to Him. Wow, I don't have *time* to be obsessed about poor treatment at an airline counter . . . even if I wanted to!

While I was focused on the ticket agent's interrogation, I didn't have even a passing thought about Jesus. The poor treatment acted like an aching tooth and consumed all my thoughts. But I looked in the Psalms and saw the text "Great peace have they which love thy law: and nothing shall offend them" (Psalm 119:105). I read about David's meditating about God both day and night. I thought about Paul's words: "I am determined not to know anything among you, save Jesus Christ, and him crucified" (1 Corinthians 2:2). And I remembered Isaiah's promise: "Thou wilt keep him in perfect peace, whose mind is stayed on thee" (Isaiah 26:3).

You know, it is a lot more fun being consumed by thoughts of Jesus. I want to be obsessed with Him. By the way, what is your obsession?

I'm No Good to Anyone

It was during the regular call that my wife, Marti, makes to her mother and father each evening at 8:00 p.m. It had not been a good day for her mother. This woman has lived a wonderful life. She was an outstanding musician and a talented teacher. She was the salesperson and kept the books for the family business. She still gets occasional calls from people who loved her when she was their junior Sabbath school teacher. But now her eyesight does not allow her to keep track of the checkbook. The beautiful church organ in the living room is usually silent because it hurts her ears. And she does not have the energy to do the cooking. In a tearful sound, it slipped out: "I'm no good to anyone. I might as well die. I am just in the way." Marti assured her mother that it is not the cooking or the teaching or the bookkeeping or the music that makes her valuable. She is valued just because she *is*. For this reason she is loved.

At graduation I asked a woman on the university campus why she had not marched in the big ceremony. "Oh, I'm not a faculty member. I am only support staff," she said. We have so many ways to tell people they are important or not important. We assign importance based on size of an office, or the length of a title—vice president, junior vice president, senior vice president, assistant vice president, first vice president, general vice president, or executive vice president. All have a shade of meaning that says you are a little more or less important than someone else.

I'm really glad that Jesus has His own system. He doesn't love just the pretty people, the best musicians, the best public speakers, the rich, or those with several degrees listed after their names. He hung around with the poor, the sick, and the outcasts. On the cross, too, the thief (the one who could do nothing for Jesus as they hung there) asked to be remembered. Jesus said, "You will be with Me in Paradise." He was a thief! But he would have received the same amount of love from Jesus if he had been a shut-in or if he had been bedridden or if he had been developmentally disabled. And it is the same for a lawyer or a physician or a member of the conference committee. Jesus doesn't love people for what they can *do* for Him. He loves people just because they *are*.

Hey, do you know what I just thought of? I'm important to Jesus. I've never been the most talented in my group, or the best looking. But it doesn't matter. God made me; I am His. Jesus loves me. Wow, what a day! I've got to go now, because I'm singing. "'Jesus loves me! this I know, for the Bible tells me so . . .'"

Oops, I came back just to tell you that Jesus loves you. You can sing too. (It doesn't even have to be in the right key.) No, it is not about what you can do for Him or how smart you are. He loves you because you *are*. Let's sing it. You at your house, and I at mine. "'Jesus loves me . . .'"

Note: Marti's mother passed away on January 3, 2000.

What I Learned When My Mother Died

Funerals are not new to me. As a pastor I've preached at many funerals and attended many more; but this one was different. This time I was sitting on the front row. This time it was for my mother. Today others too are "sitting on the front row," saying goodbye to their loved ones. Here is what I have learned about how to comfort them.

Cards and letters really are important. Stacks of them arrived from friends and fellow workers around the United States. Each one carried the *unwritten* message "I cared enough to write." Some people wrote notes of their memories of my mother. We loved to hear about her good deeds.

Within hours of her death the telephone calls started pouring in. Some people called our house while we were at the funeral home. Although we never did talk to each other on the phone, we still got the message. The girl answering the phone wrote down the names, and the message was clear: they cared enough to call. (If you ever wonder what you can do, just offer to answer the phone for the bereaved family for a few hours, keeping careful notes of who called and the message.) Only days earlier, the brother of someone I knew had died. I had wanted to call, and finally did; but I had kept putting it off because I just couldn't think of what to say. I now know that *what* you say is not nearly as important as the fact that you call.

When the flowers arrived we read each note and admired each arrangement. Especially the first ones. On our first visit to the funeral home we were tempted to wonder, *Does anyone know? Does anyone care?* But as we tiptoed into the viewing room we saw that flowers were already there!

None of us felt much like eating, much less like preparing food. The food brought to our home by friends and the meal prepared by the church were really appreciated.

Some friends left very important meetings to fly or drive for hours in order to be with us for the service. Although we didn't have much time to talk, their presence was remembered and appreciated. Now I think of it often and say to myself, "Can you imagine it! They took time to come to the funeral!"

When we returned home from the funeral in Texas, one of the pastors from our local church came to our home and comforted us with scripture and prayer. And a plant arrived at our house from our local church. We were blessed!

Others mourn today. Families are hurting because of the loss of someone they love. Jesus came "to bind up the brokenhearted . . . to comfort all that mourn" (Isaiah 61:1, 2). Cards, letters, food, calls, flowers, visits, and prayers—all help to heal the brokenhearted.

If you are alone today, thinking of the loss of your loved one, I am happy to tell you that Jesus is soon to come. He will resurrect the dead and put families together again.

Note: My mother passed away on June 1, 1997.

How to Act Like a Bride

I've never seen the Ten Commandments for Brides, but brides do have a lot in common in the way they act. They come to their weddings all fixed up with fancy white dresses. Some of those dresses are so long that they drag on the floor. Sometimes they are so long that another person has to help the bride up the steps, down the steps, into cars, and around corners. Brides also usually wear a veil and a head-piece. They don't come to the wedding in dirty tennis shoes, ragged jeans, and faded sweatshirts.

There is nothing on the marriage license that says the preacher can hear the vows only if the bride wears the pre-scribed dress. Brides just *want* to do it. It's not about getting the groom to like her. He has already committed himself to her and asked her to marry him. Neither is it about laws of marriage ceremonies. Why does the bride dress up? She wants to look beautiful to bring pleasure to the groom.

If the groom likes certain kinds of music, the bride wants to include it in the wedding program. If he likes a particular location, it will be considered in the planning for the cere-mony. The bride will even listen to his casual remarks, trying to learn what will please the one she loves.

No, the guests don't come to the ceremony to criticize the bride. She herself, however, evaluates everything, trying to bring pleasure to the groom.

Jesus says that the church is His bride. That includes me. I'm interested in acting like the bride. Yes, there are Ten

Commandments, but I don't look them over every day to make sure that I'm living up to the minimum requirements so that I don't get thrown out of heaven. My motivation is very different. When I think about Jesus and what He has done for me, I *want* to do anything I can that will bring Him pleasure, anything that might make Him happy. This has nothing to do with His acceptance of me. He has already given me salvation. But the way I look at it is this: If it is important to Him, it is important to me, even if I don't understand all about the issue. The things He has written are important to me because they tell me more about Him, about what He likes, about what He doesn't like. I learn as much as possible about Him.

Of course I dress up in the beautiful wedding garment provided by Jesus . . . getting ready to meet Him. I follow His wishes for me, not to be saved, but because I know it will make Him happy. I am not a legalist, following a check sheet to see what is right and wrong; I am a devoted lover, wanting to do everything to make my loved One happy.

Brides are like that. I want to be like that too.

Got 10 Minutes?

Have you got 10 minutes . . . just 10 minutes? Oh, it might be better if you could give more time, but even 10 minutes could make a real difference in the life of someone if you chose to spend the time for them.

Got 10 minutes? You could spend it praying for the five people to whom you most want to witness. That would mean praying for each of them for two minutes. God answers two-minute prayers!

Got 10 minutes? Sure you have. You could call one of the people on your prayer list. Say that you have only nine minutes left but that you would like to pray . . . right over the phone. You might even have a few of your 10 minutes left when you hang up.

Got 10 minutes? Why, of course you have. You could spend it writing a note to someone. The note could even include a personal testimony of your love for Jesus.

Got 10 minutes? Almost everyone does. You could spend them calling the Adventist Book Center (ABC) to order *Message* or *Signs of the Times* for someone on your prayer list. Adventists produce beautiful literature. We might as well use it often for ourselves and as gifts for others.

Got 10 minutes? Only 10? Well, you could call a friend in the hospital and wish her well, even have a short prayer with her. Sick people don't need long visits. Ten minutes will be plenty.

Got 10 minutes? Say something really positive to a young

girl or boy. A kid won't be critical if you make it a short conversation. In fact, it will probably be more comfortable for both of you if you keep it short. But 10 minutes will be enough to make a huge impact on a life.

Got 10 minutes? Everyone does. Tell a coworker what you enjoyed most in the pastor's sermon last Sabbath. In fact, you could give a very short yet good summary in much less than 10 minutes. Even a non-Christian would not have to feel pressure if you simply give a short testimony of how the pastor's sermon touched you. The first time you try it, you could even change the subject quickly—several minutes short of the 10.

Got 10 minutes? Just 10—for totally new people? Give them a leaflet about Jesus. For just the amount of money that you get paid for working 10 minutes you can buy some from the ABC. You could, in fact, give away several pieces in 10 minutes.

Got 10 minutes? Before or after church? Invite the neighbors to attend next Sabbath. Many neighbors have never been invited to attend services at our church. Could you take 10 minutes to do it?

Got 10 minutes right now? Just bow your head and pray, "Dear God, I'm spending this one minute talking to You, but I'll spend the next nine listening to what You would like to tell me. What would You like to say to me if I would only be still? Are there any jobs You need me to do? OK, God, I'm Yours, and my time is Yours. I'm listening."

Criticism Is Not a
Fruit of the Spirit

Criticism is not one of the fruits of the Spirit. Even constructive criticism is not mentioned in the Bible as one of the special characteristics of a person filled with the Holy Spirit. Jesus never said, "Blessed are those who criticize, because they perform a wonderful ministry." However, it does sometimes appear that when wrongs are evident, sin does need to be called by its right name.

The Israelites had just succeeded in conquering the land of Canaan. It was obvious to all of them that God had been leading. He had told them to cross the Jordan, and He had stopped the flow of the river to make it possible to cross to the other side. He had given instruction to bring 12 stones from the center of the river and to construct an altar as a reminder of what God had done for them. God had destroyed the first city the Israelites encountered after they followed His instructions to march around it, blow their horns, and shout. As they did what God commanded, He worked miracles for them.

But some warriors went back to the other side of the river and built another altar. How could they have done this? They ought to have known that God would not allow such a thing; after all, they had been instructed to tear down the altars of the heathen. How could it be that now some of the leaders seemed to be acting in opposition to God's commands? They appeared to be acting like the heathen and building their own altar. With the true followers of God there was concern, then muttering, then agitated gossiping, and finally open criticism.

Eventually it was agreed that these rebellious, adulterous tribes would need to be taught a lesson. Fortunately, before engaging in war, someone decided to go and ask the rebels for an explanation.

Those who had built the altar said: "Wait! We are not worshiping another God. We put the altar up to remind us that all 12 tribes are one, and that the people on this side of the river should remember what God has done for us. It is similar to the altar on the other side reminding us of God."

Most of the time when we criticize, the matter is really not any of our business. We should simply be an example of serving God ourselves. But on those rare occasions when we must criticize, we at least ought to talk to those who seem to be in error. They might have a good explanation for what we are criticizing.

A few years ago Willard Regester of California started the Aaron and Hur Club. It is made up of people who have pledged to refrain from criticizing the leadership of the church and to hold them up before God in prayer, as Aaron and Hur held up the arms of Moses during battle.

At many campfires we have sung with great fervor, "Oh, give me a home, where the buffalo roam, where the deer and the antelope play; where seldom is heard a discouraging word . . ." Wouldn't it be wonderful to be in a place where we didn't hear any discouraging words or criticism?

Let's try it. If we are afraid we can't make it for a whole week, let's ask God to help us for today. Just today let's speak only positive things, only encouraging words. Jesus Himself will be willing to help us do it.

"Set a watch, O Lord, before my mouth; keep the door of my lips" (Psalm 141:3).

No, Thanks,
Maybe Tomorrow

It seems strange to me. I saved him several thousand dollars, yet he never even said thank you. I didn't do the favor for him to get recognition. I did it because I wanted to do it, and because I thought it was the right thing to do. There was a cost, and it was inconvenient. But I was sure that it was the right thing, so I did it. Now I wonder why the man never even mentioned it. Did he not recognize it as a favor or a gift? Is it something that he has just come to expect, so that he sees no need to acknowledge it? Has he been too busy?

Then I got to thinking about what Jesus does for me . . . every day. How often do I tell *Him* thank You? Do you suppose that He is wondering if I've even noticed what He has done for me? His gifts come so regularly to me that it would not be impossible for me to expect them to always be there. Every day I wake up, right? And I have a good place to live. Every day I have food to eat. And every day I enjoy good health. These gifts have become so commonplace that I'm sure I don't say thank You to Jesus often enough.

Maybe He is trying to excuse my thoughtlessness. Maybe He says, "Oh, when he wakes up he will talk to Me." But then that day things get so busy that I hardly say hello.

So He might be saying, "Toward the middle of the day maybe Don will spend a little time with Me. Maybe he'll read some of My Letter to him. Surely then he'll talk to Me and just say thanks for so many things." But during the middle of the day I have so many *important* appointments and meetings that I only say the same prayer at mealtime that I've said many times before. It was a habit and not really meaningful, neither to Jesus nor to me.

Do you suppose that He says, "Well, at the end of the day we will have a little time together"? But then I come to the end of the day, and I've worked all day, and I'm so tired. I fall asleep right away, and still I haven't really talked with Jesus to tell Him thank You for salvation, for family, for friends, for safety, and for so many other things. Probably He is wondering if I've even noticed what He's done for me. What Jesus did for me He did because He wanted to, and because He felt that it was right to do, but a thank You wouldn't hurt.

So right now I am going to take some time to actually do it. Yes, I have other things awaiting my attention, and I am in a great hurry; but I want Jesus to know that I *really* believe that He's important to me. I'm stopping my other activities right now for a while to say thank You to Jesus.

"Thank You for salvation; and thank You for my family. Thank You for health. Thank You for this new day. . . . Thank You, Jesus!"

People Who Prayed for Me

P ray for me." I've heard many people make this request. Sometimes I've said it myself.

And, of course, I agree to pray for people. Usually I do; however, many times I have agreed to—and meant to—but got busy with other things and forgotten their request. Now I'm trying to remember to pray with everyone who requests it, and many who have not even thought of suggesting it.

Jesus said, "If you want anything, just ask Me." We are assured that where two or three of us are together, Jesus is there. Just think of it. When we are with our friends, we can all talk to Him. I just love the idea of having Jesus as a part of our discussion. He is, after all, the best friend that I have. Sometimes when I talk to my other friends, they don't even listen, but Jesus assures us that He will always listen and answer.

Wouldn't it be wonderful if our church was known for the fact that we pray often and regularly for and with each other?

As I was about to begin my ministry in the Lake Union, I agreed to meet Norm Klam, the Lake Union treasurer, to discuss some issues we would face. At the time, we were both traveling and met at a motel. When Norm came to my room he said, "Before we discuss even the first issue, I want to pray for you." We knelt in the motel room and prayed together that God would be in charge of our ministry.

On my first day at the Lake Union office I stayed late into the night. I heard a loud noise. Someone was knocking on the outside door. When I opened the door, I found Dwight

Nelson, pastor of the Pioneer Memorial church in Berrien Springs, Michigan. He had been attending a meeting at the church. Dwight stated: "I saw your light, and just wanted to stop to pray for you." He didn't spend long, but we knelt together as he prayed for me and my ministry.

On another day a worker in the office was talking with me about a difficult subject. He said, "I don't know what the answer to this question is, but I want to kneel here with you and pray for you."

I believe that if each of us were to choose just one person each week and consistently pray for that person, it would transform our church. Or what if people who are confined to their homes would daily call someone on a church list just to say "I've been thinking of you today and praying for you; now I'd like to pray together with you"?

A veterinarian in Colorado was examining my friend's dog. The veterinarian said, "I'll need to operate on your dog, but before we do, let's pray together." The boy loved his dog, and the veterinarian was a strong witness to him. What if everyone in a health-care field prayed with all of their patients before leaving them?

I think God would be pleased to have us talking to Him when we are with our friends. He invites us to come to Him anytime—even right now.

A Different Kind of Hero

"Two, four, six, eight . . . who do we appreciate?" Usually we hear the chant at a sporting event. Then the name of a player in the game is yelled out—the player who has just scored several points, perhaps. The crowd is showing appreciation for the hero of the game.

Today I am thinking about a different kind of hero. But I'm not talking about the presidents of our conferences or hospitals or colleges and universities or publishing houses. I'm not talking about our well-known evangelists who work so tirelessly to bring people to Jesus. I'm not talking about people who are able to give large amounts of money to advance God's cause, and whose names are rightly recognized for the way God has been able to work through them.

No, I'm talking about other heroes, and mostly I don't even know their names. But they are very important, people who deserve our thanks and appreciation. I'm talking about church secretaries, Sabbath school teachers, Community Services volunteers, Home and School coordinators, deacons and deaconesses who mow the lawn, wash the Communion cups and fold the linen, fix the furnace and clean up flooded church basements. There are even students on some of our college campuses whose job it is just to change thousands of lightbulbs or just repair vacuum cleaners. And I appreciate them. How irritating it would be if someone wasn't conscientiously looking after important things like that.

Sometimes people tell me that they appreciate things I

have written and published in our papers. And yet I'm only partly responsible for them. After I write, editors fix it up, and the press operators at the printing plants do their vital work, and then clean up the mess.

It takes more than a good preacher to make a church successful. One church I pastored attracted several new members just because of the excellent cradle roll Sabbath school program.

Two, four, six, eight . . . who do I appreciate? It's all these people whose names will never be widely recognized, who likely will not be in the news—the people who contribute so much to our churches, schools, and towns. I say, "Thanks to all of you for the way you bless others, and thanks for being willing to work without credit or glory. In God's plan all are equally important, no matter what our job titles."

Two, four, six, eight . . . who do I appreciate? *You!* Y-e-a-h!

I'm a Very Important Person

I tell you, I am a very important person. Not because of the one I married, or because of my name or title or job, or because of what I own. But it is true just the same—I am a very important person.

The reason is that I was created in the image of God (Genesis 1:26, 27), and God doesn't look too kindly on anyone calling something He has made common or unclean (Acts 10:28). I once saw a sign that read "I'm somebody, 'cause God don't make no junk!" Because He made me, I am very important.

I'm also important because He died for me. The God of heaven valued me so much that He devised a plan so that He could take me to live with Him forever, a plan that meant, however, that He would die. Surely it is hard to believe, but it is true—He died for me. He wouldn't leave heaven and take the guff that He took except for a very good reason. I was that reason! That alone makes me somebody special—a very important person.

I've got an important job, and *that* makes me important. I'm not referring to an elected position. I mean that God has a plan for my *life* (*Christ's Object Lessons*, p. 326), a special work for me to do. He didn't simply allow me to be born and then say to me, "Do whatever you can." He has *a work* for me. I feel really important—and humbled—when I think that God would like to use me.

He made only one like me. I'm special, unique, important.

(I know some who read this will say, "Good! I'm glad He made only one of those.") Jesus has only one kind of each of us. So when I am gone there will be no other just like me. Like an original piece of art, one of a kind.

Jesus is my brother! Think of the way we pay attention to the president's family. We even give honor to his brothers or sisters. Well, my brother is Jesus. He even claims me and is willing to stand openly with me. To have a brother like Him—that really makes me important.

I am very important—to Jesus. It humbles me to realize what attention and effort and love Jesus has invested in me, in you. And because He has done so much for me, I can't help wanting to serve Him today.

Adventists Should Act Like We're From the Ritz-Carlton

Jesus and I are friends. I have experienced His forgiveness and have found in Him power to live the Christian life. This friendship leads me to look eagerly into His Word to see what He has in mind for me. While Jesus was living here on this earth, He said many things, important things, about how He wanted His friends to live and act.

I especially notice Jesus' attitude toward people. We read of His compassion for the multitudes. His instructions often dealt with the way we as His disciples treat others. He said that a good way to check on yourself is to "do unto others as you want them to do unto you" (see Matthew 7:12). He counseled us to put other people ahead of ourselves. And He especially warned that we not hurt little children by the things we say and do, declaring that it would be better for a millstone to be hung around our neck and we be put into the water than for us to hurt one of the little ones.

Then, too, I read that Jesus has given us the assignment of telling everyone that He is coming to get His friends and inviting them to get to know Him. It is a wonderful privilege and a great responsibility. Jesus says in Acts 1:8 that we should start by telling those close to us about Him—then those in our town, our state, our country, and then in the entire world.

The motto for the employees of the Ritz-Carlton Hotel chain says, "We are ladies and gentlemen serving ladies and gentlemen." And while the hotel guests love the beautiful rooms, swimming pools, and lobbies, they mostly comment on the service.

We are all God's special people. Our motto can be "We are sons and daughters of God serving other sons and daughters of God." Every person we meet is a person for whom Jesus died. They are special to Him. Jesus loves that one—even when they dress incorrectly, smell bad, and drink things that are bad for them.

Jesus said, "I am coming back to take you into My kingdom if you take special care of the people I love—if you've fed the hungry, visited the people in prison, and taken care of the homeless." Sounds as though He places a lot of importance on this subject, doesn't it?

Today I challenge you—and myself—to look at every person as one of those people for whom Jesus died. We can do it with our offerings, our attitudes, our actions, and our words.

What's Good About Our Church?

Magazines often come to my desk that specialize in what is wrong with the church. I have not felt called to the ministry of tearing down the church, or calling attention to what is wrong with the church. In fact, I'd like to tell you some things that I think are *good* about the church.

1. *It preaches about Jesus.* Our church produces Christ-centered media programs, literature, and sermons every day. I want to make sure that church members talk about Jesus, so I'm reminding myself right now to do it. The Adventist Church is the most Christ-centered church I've ever heard of.

2. *The church is growing.* It took us 97 years to reach our first million members, but in 2000 we added just over a million, and the total membership now is more than 11 million.

3. *The church encourages education.* My aunts and uncles did not accept this message, and none of them were privileged to get the type of education I received. One of the main differences is this church. We talk about preparing for greater service, and education is a big part of that. Adventist members are among the most educated in the world. Imagine a city in the United States with a population of 900,000 supporting the number of church-sponsored colleges and universities that we operate—in addition to supporting public education.

4. *The church encourages healthful living.* You can hardly find an Adventist magazine that does not offer some suggestion for healthful living. All this contributes to the average Adventist

living seven years longer than the average population.

5. *The church is making bold attempts to spread the message about the return of Jesus.* Millions of people have been reached and scores of thousands have been baptized through the explosion of satellite evangelism programs the church has sponsored all around the world.

6. *The church urges its members to be compassionate.* Corporately and personally. Thousands of people were helped by our Community Services centers last year.

7. *The church is big business.* It owns thousands of pieces of property and has thousands of employees who handle millions of dollars. Once in a while something goes wrong with an investment. This happens so rarely that it makes big news. People talk about it for years, and some publications devote many pages to the discussion. Yet almost every day correct business decisions are being made, and thousands of employees are doing their jobs properly.

8. *This church is organized to help members and nonmembers find Jesus.* I'm thankful for the Adventist Church. It has made a difference in my life.

Have You Been Hurt?

Have you been hurt by someone in the church? Did someone say something to you that still causes you pain? Or did someone talk about you? Do you feel you deserve an apology, but that individual will not ask for your forgiveness?

Have you been having a difficult time with the church because of that person's actions? And are you even having a difficult time being close to Jesus because of what someone has done? Then I'm writing this to you.

I apologize for the distress you have experienced. I am sorry for what has happened. Please accept my apology! I want to invite you into a new relationship with Jesus. Sometimes His followers don't do well representing Him. They say and do the wrong things. We saw it among the disciples who walked in His footsteps, and we see it today. I'm sorry that you have been hurt. I neither justify nor excuse it; I'm simply saying that I'm sorry, and I'm asking you to forgive.

David and his army of trained men had been camped near Nabal's home and had been protecting Nabal's farm. When the men needed food, David asked some of his men to approach Nabal, asking him for whatever he could spare. Nabal was impolite and unkind to the messengers, and he sent them away with nothing. Anger filled David so that he determined to kill Nabal and his men. David took 400 soldiers with him to do the job. On the way he came upon Abigail, Nabal's wife. She had heard how her husband had been so unkind and unappreciative of David, and she went to apologize.

She reminded God's anointed that he, David, was not a vengeful person, and begged him to let God bless him and take care of his enemies. It was good advice. David had been planning to kill innocent people in order to get even. But David did not pursue Nabal. He dropped the whole matter because of Abigail's apology.

Abigail's advice is good for us, too. Let's not make our forgiveness dependent on the actions of any other person. God can and will deal with them. Our happiness should not be controlled by another's good or bad actions. Their failure to confess must not be used as a reason for our failure to forgive.

If someone has hurt you, please allow Jesus to deal with that person. Let's invite Him into our heart again—to give us a forgiving heart and to bring His happiness into our life. No good can come by waiting to forgive.

Before He died, Jesus forgave the men who put Him to death. So that He could forgive us, Jesus died for us while we were yet sinners. We can forgive others while they are yet sinners too. Then the happiness that Jesus brings can light up our lives.

Please Accept Me

Please accept me. I want to be needed. I want to be wanted. Oh, yes, accept me *just the way I am* . . . and let me be involved."

I was listening to a focus group of young adults who were talking to me about the church. Some of their friends had gone to churches and been turned off, they said, just because of the members' reactions to their hairstyle or clothing choice (or so it *seemed* to them). The young adults in my office were not being critical. They were simply pleading with me to help them or someone bring about changes so that young people would feel good about the church and would be more involved. "Some of our friends are not attending anymore," they told me.

Then I thought of another focus group that I had attended about two months earlier. The woman talking was 85 years of age. She and her husband had moved to a new community because they needed some assistance; their children could provide transportation to the store, to church, or to the doctor. But in the previous community they left behind the church where she had been the organist for nearly 40 years and where he had been an elder or a deacon many of those years. Now they spent most Sabbaths at home watching the services on TV. She was speaking for herself and other 85-year-olds. "We want to be involved," she said in a halting voice. "I know we can't do the things we once did, but is there any way we could be a part of the church just the way we are? We would like to contribute our talents. Is there anything for which we are needed at the church? Sometimes we feel as though no one in the church cares about us."

To me it sounded like an echo of a middle-aged professional woman in California who had just moved into a new community, leaving behind old church offices and friends. And it was the same message expressed by a widow: "Most church meetings are for people who have a husband. I'm alone, and I feel it. I wish I could feel more accepted. I wish I could feel that the church would like to use me even though I'm alone."

Actually it is the same for me, too. I want to be accepted. I want to be needed. I want to be wanted, just like the young adults, just like the 85-year-old woman, like the middle-aged professional woman and the widow. The truth is, all of us are special to Jesus. He loves and needs us all.

Dear Jesus, I want to be more accepting of the young adults—hairstyles, fashions, music, and all. And I want to pay extra attention to the elderly—hairstyles, fashions, music, and all. Make me aware of the needs of the others, too. Let me understand how fragile all Your people are and how much encouragement each one needs. Lord, let me live out Your love and Your acceptance.

Angels Couldn't Do It

A ngels couldn't do it, so people did.

It seemed almost like blasphemy to me, too, when I first heard the man say it. I would not have accepted it either, but he started reading from *The Desire of Ages* (p. 297). I listened; then I read it for myself.

The man told me about his separation from God. He'd been disappointed, estranged, even angry with God. People had been praying for him. And there is no doubt in my mind that God was calling him back. But even with all that the Holy Spirit was doing, neither the man nor his wife made a recommitment to the Saviour.

Then one of the workers from our office knocked on his door. During the visit this worker told about the love of Jesus. It wasn't anything new; the man had heard it many times before. In fact, he had told that very gospel story again and again, but now he needed to hear it himself. And during that visit he accepted Jesus all over again. Some days later when I visited, I heard his wife confide that she too wanted to be a friend of Jesus again.

That's when the man took me aside and told me that both he and his wife had needed to see a person. They had not been able to make a commitment to God with only the wooing of the Holy Spirit. And he read to me, "There are souls perplexed with doubt, burdened with infirmities, weak in the faith, and unable to grasp the Unseen; but a friend whom they can see, coming to them in Christ's stead, can be a connecting link to fasten their trembling faith upon Christ."

That's what we were! Not anything special. Not highly talented professionals. Just friends who turned out to be connecting links. The angels would have been happy to do it, but they couldn't.

The man said that God had not been able to get through to him. Neither could the angels. What was required was another human being—one who also was weak, but who had felt the power of God.

It doesn't seem right, and surely we can't boast about it, but sometimes God can't even use the angels as effectively as He can use us. What an awesome thought! I'm going to give myself to God again right now and tell Him that if He needs me, if I can do something that angels can't do, or if I can do *anything at all* for Him, to just go ahead and use me. I'm praying, "Here am I; send me" (Isaiah 6:8).

I Was in Prison

It didn't look like a prison, but I felt as if I were in one. I didn't do anything bad to be forced to spending time in that place. I volunteered. It looked like any other house on the street. There was a car in the garage, an almost-new pickup in the driveway, and the keys were on the table. It would have been possible to leave anytime, but I just couldn't. Like other prisons, the food was prescribed for me. I ate what people brought or what I fixed from the supplies I found in the cupboard, but I didn't go to the store for groceries. Oh, I had the money to buy food and a way to get to the store, but I couldn't go. I couldn't even take a shower when I wanted to.

I was with my father. He had lived alone since my mother's death six months earlier, and now he was dying. It could have happened any day. The cancer had almost won the battle, but he was still fighting back. He had not been out of bed for five days, and sometimes he wondered where he was. It took a lot of medication for him to withstand the pain.

Because he called for me occasionally, and because the phone might ring, I stayed in his bedroom, in the kitchen, or in the living room only a few steps away. I didn't even walk out to the street to get the mail unless there was someone to answer his call or pick up the phone before he panicked.

Joe, the neighbor, was wonderful. He had been in a motorcycle accident and couldn't drive a car or work at a regular job, but he wanted to be helpful. He came at regular times. One morning at 10:00 I asked him to listen for the phone and for my father's calls while I took a shower. It was wonderful! As I stood in the shower I was a free man again. Then I took time to shave. The 10 minutes that Joe was there gave me a new lease on life. I felt that I could make it for the rest of the day, just because of his 10-minute gift.

It doesn't take a lot of skill to do what Joe did for me and for my father. Almost anyone can do it. Just go to the caregiver at a sick person's home. Say, "I'll be here for 10 minutes or 30 minutes or whatever, *and you go* do what you want. I'll sit here by the sick person and not talk to you or him; I'll just be here, and you do as you wish."

In every neighborhood there are people in prison. Look for them. Just a few minutes will make a big difference. Every church has elderly members. Some young mothers with babies at home are glad to be caring for their children but sometimes feel so confined. A break for them may be the highlight of their week.

Jesus said that true religion is visiting the sick and those in prison. I sure can understand why it is important.

Where Adolf Hitler Died

I went to the place where it happened. It was difficult to find. No historical marker designated the spot. People around weren't interested. For them it was a nonstory too. I didn't take a snapshot. That is why no picture goes with this nonstory.

Our country sets markers where special events have taken place. We make statues to remind us of people connected to these events. There in Germany, where I was visiting, the same is true. Markers, signposts, statues, and churches of every description notified us of places of historical importance. At most of these sites I could buy books or videos or picture postcards to remind me of my visit.

But it was different where I stood *that* day. Not a marker, not a signpost, not a picture could be found . . . a field full of weeds was all that I saw. As I said, it was a nonstory, so of course, there were no pictures. After some research, though, I could tell I was at the right place. It certainly was a nonstory!

Just a couple hours south of where I was standing, the home, the church, and the life of Martin Luther are well documented. But then, he made a difference . . . for God. He wrote, he preached, he believed that Jesus' life and death make possible our right relationship with God. Of course, he made mistakes, but he set out to make a difference for *God*. Today visitors come constantly to the church where he preached and look for the door of the church where he nailed the 95 theses. His is an exciting story known by people around the world—

this story of Martin Luther and the little town of Wittenberg with its then only 2,500 inhabitants.

But there I stood in Berlin looking at weeds in a vacant lot. There, you see, Adolf Hitler died. At one time he was one of the most powerful men on the face of the earth, yet no marker shows the spot where he died. No visitor's center tells where his bunker stood. Tourists don't come here by the busload to take pictures. No postcards are available. Not even a gravestone can be seen. Just weeds. There *is* no wonderful story. Most people in the neighborhood just want to forget what happened here. For them it is a nonstory, and no special pictures accompany this nonstory. Anyway, who would want a picture of a bunch of weeds on a vacant lot?

What makes the difference between the story and the nonstory? Jesus . . . serving Jesus! Hitler and Luther were both leaders. Both were gifted speakers. Both influenced many people. But serving Jesus made the difference.

Do I want my life to count? Yes! Do I want to make a difference? Definitely! The only way that I can be sure of accomplishing something lasting is to give my life to Jesus. And at this moment I'm doing that again.

Ever Heard of Palti and Gaddi?

C an I make a difference?" This was one of my main questions as I thought about accepting the call to broader church responsibility. I didn't want to move just to have a different position or simply to live in a different location. As I sought the counsel of several people and asked God to show me His will, the big question was "Can I make a difference if I accept the position?"

Sometimes when my wife, Marti, and I are praying together, I pray, "Lord, please help us to make a difference for You today." I don't want just to go through the motions. One time I was gone from home for a few days attending meetings. When I called home, Marti asked, "Did you make a difference today, or were you just at the meetings?"

Trustee is a magazine published for hospital governing boards. I read an article in that magazine once that talked about the qualities of an outstanding leader. Even though this magazine does not claim to be a spiritually oriented publication, it declared, "The most significant factor contributing to outstanding leadership is the executive's strong inner core of spirituality consisting of two competencies: faith in God and finding meaning in the events of everyday life." The study showed empirically that spirituality explains 65 percent of the differences between outstanding and average performance.

What does this tell us? It is yet another reminder that if you want to make a difference for God, you must stay close to Him, developing your faith in Him. What kind of job or profession you have does not make the significant difference. Your relationship with Jesus is what makes the difference—your allowing Him to live in you and speak and work through you.

Have you heard of Palti and Gaddi? These were outstanding leaders in the Bible, chosen from among their peers to represent their tribes (Numbers 13:4-15). These men worked hard at their assigned job. They did their best to give what they assumed was good advice. However, these men forgot to trust God. They needed to seek God's wisdom and power, and to depend on Him.

Because Palti and Gaddi depended on their human reasoning and methods instead of God's guidance, most of us have never heard of them. These men did not make a positive impact for God. In fact, in spite of their hard work, their decisions caused great misery and suffering for their families. You see, they were a part of the group sent to spy out the land of Canaan. They saw the reality of the wonderful land, but they also saw the reality of the gigantic inhabitants. They said, "They are stronger than we" (verse 31). And it was true.

But how many of us remember Caleb and Joshua? We remember them because they trusted God in the face of great difficulties. These two men testified to their faith, "The Lord is with us: fear them not" (Numbers 14:9). And their testimony lives on for us. Will we make a positive difference for God as did Caleb and Joshua?

The best suggestion I have for you is "Stay close to Jesus, and your life will make a difference for Him."

Why I Never Find Agates

Jesus said, "Go! Tell people! Teach them, and baptize them." What have we been doing with this command? Oh, I'm not talking about the corporate church. This is not a discussion of how the Adventist message is doing in new countries; nor am I seeking a global mission report. I am merely asking how things are going in the neighborhood in which you live? How well do I know my neighbors? Do they know that Jesus is coming? Have I told them? Have you told yours?

Has anyone ever said to you, "Thank you for introducing me to Jesus"? Will anyone be able to say to you in heaven, "I am here because you gave me the invitation"? I want to do my best to help people know about Jesus and the good news of His return. I want to do that because Jesus and I are friends. It's so wonderful knowing Him that I want *everyone* to know about Him too and experience the joy of serving Him. But beyond that, I recognize it is my obligation as a Christian to be a missionary for Jesus.

Some things in life simply happen, but most events require conscious effort. I challenge you to put thought and effort into the idea of being a witness for Jesus.

For several years I worked at Camp Yorktown Bay, a youth camp in Arkansas. E. Frank Sherrill, who was then the conference president, would come to visit. As we walked across the campus together he would often stop, pick up an object, and say to me, "Here is an agate." It happened every few feet. The curious thing is that I never found a single agate in all the years that I was at the camp. I'm sure the reason for this was that I haven't the slightest interest in agates, and so looking for them had not been an overwhelming passion for me. Likewise, I believe some of us have never developed an interest in searching out people to invite to heaven, and so we have never looked for them. But now I'm inviting *you* to think about the people you know whom you might speak to about Jesus—people you might influence under the guidance of the Holy Spirit.

I think it would be good to pray: "Lord, help me to be an effective witness for You. Help me to find people who will listen to the message about Jesus." If you ask Jesus to help you find someone who will be ready to receive your witness, I believe that God will place you with the right person.

Try making a prayer list, not just of people who are missionaries in foreign fields, but also those closer to home—a list of those whom you hope to influence for Jesus. Make a list of people you are likely to see over the next few weeks. Then ask God to help you witness to them in the most effective manner. I believe that He will direct your thoughts, words, and actions.

Witnessing isn't only for a few skilled professionals. Witnessing is for *everyone*. In fact, we are all witnessing all of the time in some manner or another, whether we like it or not. The question is, then, "Am I witnessing for God, or not?"

Today I want my witness to be positive and intentional for Jesus. Someday very soon He'll be returning. And when He does, I want to be able to look forward to meeting the people who have been brought to Jesus through my life and words. Today let's ask God to help us be His mouthpiece wherever He needs us.

Don't Ask God for Anything

Could I borrow 50 bucks?" It was my friend again. On other occasions he had asked me for a ride, for the use of my car, and for help getting a job. He had asked for a lot of things, but I really don't remember a time when he called just to say hello or to tell me thanks for the things I'd already done for him.

I wonder, does Jesus ever have similar thoughts? Do you suppose that He ever says, "Gabriel, I don't ever remember that person praying for any reason other than to ask Me for favors. He has asked for help with the marriage, for help with the kids, and for help with buying or selling something. But he never just says, 'Thanks for the good day,' or 'Thanks for what You did yesterday.' "

Some years ago the Heritage Singers sang a song that said, "I have not come to ask for anything. I've just come to talk with You, Lord." What if we tried praying like that sometime? Just say, "Dear God, I didn't come to ask for things this time; this time, I've just come to thank You." And then list things, large and small, for which we want to thank God— things He has done, things He has provided for us.

He does say in the Bible that we should come to Him asking things in His name, but there are also many texts that say, "Praise the Lord," or "Give thanks to God." We've probably all lodged more requests than praises. What would it do for God if we doubled the number of praises and halved the requests? What would it do for our own attitude?

Today during one of my prayer times with God I'm not going to ask for anything. I'm just going to think about all the things He's done for me already, and I'm going to thank Him. Then I'm going to spend some time thinking about who our God really is and praising Him. There has been a precedent established for this. David did it. Some of his psalms are made up of only praise. What if we would set aside the first day of each month to send only praises and thanks to God. Let's try it. Right now tell Him thank You for several things.

Party Time in Heaven

It was party time in heaven with a lot of smiles, a lot of happiness, and a lot of rejoicing. I don't know just how parties are done in heaven, but maybe the angels were jumping up and down, hugging each other, some slapping each other on the back, shaking hands, with some high fives mixed in.

There were several names connected with the big celebration, a lot of them angels. But there were two names on everyone's lips. Jesus was one. There would be no party without Him. He made it all possible. I think I can almost hear Him saying, "Wow, it was worth it all after all!" The other name connected with the celebration was my name—and I didn't even attend. But it was when my name came up that the party began.

Jesus gave the setting for this when He told the stories that are now in Luke 15. I really like the one about the sheep that was lost. The Owner (that was Jesus Himself) went looking for it. He says that when He found it, He picked it up and brought it back, inviting the neighbors over to join Him and His friends for a celebration. Jesus said, "That is the way it works in heaven, too. There is real rejoicing when a sinner comes to Jesus."

When my name came up in heaven, the angels had been talking about me, the rascal who didn't seem to have any interest in serving Jesus. Then I made a decision to allow Jesus to forgive my sins. He was happy! After all, this is why He died.

And the angels were happy, because they really wanted me to serve Jesus. That's when the party broke out . . . when the news hit heaven that I had decided to give my life to Jesus.

They had a party for you, too. Or if not, they certainly would like to have one. They know that serving Jesus brings happiness. Jesus died so that He could forgive you. Jesus has dealt with a lot of other big-time sinners . . . and forgiven them, too. He *will* do it for you. How can this happen? Just bow your head, invite Jesus into your life, and let the party in heaven begin. I can imagine someone shouting, "*[your name]* has accepted the grace of Jesus. Whoopee! Let's celebrate and thank Jesus for making it possible."

Worship Is Our Gift to God

Worship is our gift to our God. Because we are giving this present to Him, we want to make sure that it is what He likes.

At Christmastime we go to the mall and purchase presents for those we love. Always the first question must be "What would bring her the most pleasure? What would he enjoy?" I do not give my son a new dress shirt, even though he might need one. I have given him the same Christmas gift for many years—a ticket to go downhill skiing. That is something he really enjoys.

As for me, I enjoy tools. I can make a visit to the tool section of Sears and almost start drooling. At Christmas some years ago I gave a set of 24 screwdrivers to a man who said, "Thank you, but I already have a screwdriver." I couldn't understand. I want more—short ones, long ones, fat ones, skinny ones. But he had no interest in tools. He didn't really enjoy the gift.

When we give the gift of worship, the first question must be "What would God enjoy?" Have you noticed that we often start by asking, "How would I like it best?" "How would our youth like it?" or "How would our older members like our Sabbath service?" The real question is "How would God like it best?"

God does seem to be particular about worship. He told Moses to take off his shoes at the burning bush because the ground on which he was standing was holy. He wanted the incense offered in the tabernacle in only certain ways—even saying that some fire that Nadab and Abihu used was unacceptable. They died because they worshiped the way that pleased themselves.

David prayed, "Let the words of my mouth, and the meditation of my heart, be acceptable in thy sight, O Lord" (Psalm 19:14). When I worship on Sabbath morning (and during other worships, too), I am going to sing with my whole heart, as do the angels, conscious that I sing to the glory and for the pleasure of my Saviour. I will pray and give and read Scripture—in fact, do all—to the glory of God. I want to be sure that my heart is bound up with my gift of worship. I want to send it with love.

Dear Jesus, "let the words of my mouth, and the meditation of my heart, be acceptable in thy sight."

New Members Can Cause Problems

We were overjoyed with the news. Our long-awaited, prayed-for new family member was soon to be born. Friends gave us presents. We bought furniture designed especially for babies. We even redecorated a bedroom.

But when he arrived, wow! Did he ever create a lot of problems! He didn't speak our language, didn't eat the kind of food we ate, and didn't want to sleep when we wanted to sleep. He wouldn't even dress himself. Mostly he seemed interested in eating, crying, and creating messes. But strange as it may sound, we were thrilled to have him!

We have been praying for new members and have spent many dollars preparing for them. We are thrilled that God is answering our prayers as record numbers join the church—more than at any time in the history of the church in North America—but we can expect to have some stress.

Marti and I were in the family years before our babies arrived, but we had to make many adjustments . . . and so it is in the church. New people may sit right where the regular members have been sitting for years. They may not bring the right food to potlucks and may not even dress *correctly* or use the right language. Join me in praying that God will give us the grace to treat the new people the very way Jesus would treat them.

We didn't expect much of our new babies—and it's a good thing, too! New additions to the family or church need a lot of help and support, not criticism, even the constructive kind. If they do need correction, it is best done by the ones who have brought them into the family. When you see new members needing correction, ask yourself some questions: Have I been their main prayer support as they were coming into this church? Did I give them Bible studies? Would they consider me their closest friend in the church? If you are not the person responsible for introducing them to Jesus, probably you are not the best person to correct them. *A note of caution:* if parents react too severely when children make mistakes, we call it child abuse. Surely there will be no cases of abuse of new members in the church.

My son walks just like I walk, but I never have discussed the theory of walking with him. He learned by watching and trying for himself. New members learn that way too. They can learn about family worship, for instance, by being in a member's home at sundown Sabbath evening.

As parents have responsibility for their children, I believe that we all have responsibility for the new people coming to the church, too. Let's pray, pray, and pray some more . . . for them and for ourselves. Pray that God will protect and strengthen our new members. And pray that we will take such good care of them that they will be glad they joined our family.

You Cannot Not Witness!

Everybody is doing it . . . all the time. It really does not take any training to do it. Nor is it the kind of thing where an individual at the podium in a public meeting says, "By the authority invested in me and because you have met the requirements, I now pronounce you a witness." No. God said, "Ye are my witnesses" (Isaiah 43:10; Acts 1:8). And . . . we all *are* His witnesses. But just as it is in court, there are witnesses *for* Him and witnesses *against* Him. Either way, though, we are witnesses.

We are witnesses all the time. From the time we see the first person in the morning until our day is over, we are witnesses. Everything we do, everything we say (even some things we didn't intend to say), and the way we act—all are a part of our witness. It is not something we turn on or off or that we plan to do at 3:00 on Sabbath afternoon. Being a witness is a 24-hour-a-day thing—all day, every day.

Some of us say we are afraid to witness, but afraid or confident, we are still His witnesses.

The issue is not *Will you be a witness?* The question is *What kind of witness will you be? Will your witness be for Jesus or against Him?*

People judge Jesus by looking at those of us who are called by His name. I believe our witness deserves some conscious thought. What we do and say will influence someone for Jesus. Will that person think more of Jesus or less of Him because of a contact with us?

Witnessing is really quite natural. When a person is in love with Jesus, it shows, and others see it. But those who want to witness for Him will look for extra openings to slip testimonies about Him into the conversation. It is similar to a bride who is preparing for her wedding. She slips that topic into almost any conversation. Soon people figure out that she is in love.

So my concern is not whether I am a witness, but rather, *Can people see the real Jesus through me?* At this moment I am asking Him to make me a witness that speaks for Him and not against Him. I want Him to control all of my words and actions so that people will be closer to Him because of their being with me.

Everybody is witnessing all the time. I want my witness to be in His favor!

Her Did What Her Could

erita was only 4 when she stayed in our home for a week while her mother was sick. We did our best to take the place of her parents and regularly studied her Sabbath school lesson with her. The memory verse for that week was "She hath done what she could" (Mark 14:8). Jesus Himself had spoken the words when Mary anointed Him with perfume. Although Judas complained that Mary had wasted money, Jesus had no criticism for Mary. And He didn't mention that she couldn't preach repentance like Peter or expound theology like Paul. He just said that she had done what she *could do*.

When her parents came to get her, we proudly asked little Serita to say the memory verse for them. With an intent expression and a deep breath she said, "Her did what her could." Did we criticize her English? No! We praised her for getting the message of the story correct. Serita too had done what she could.

Jesus accepts our simple gifts when they are our best. When I attended a meeting at a church in Illinois, I heard the children's choir sing. Later the director told me that she cannot play the piano, does not understand 3/4 or 4/4 time, and cannot even read notes. What she knows is that the kids of the church need to be involved in as many ways as possible. That is why she decided to start a choir. She bought a few tapes of music and asked the kids to sing along. The kids were happy, the audience was happy, and I believe the words of Jesus, as quoted by Serita, are fitting: "Her did what her could."

At the same church I met the director of the Community Services center, who works from her wheelchair. She told me that she knows what it is like to be in need. Her husband had been laid off from Caterpillar a few years before. At that time she stood in line waiting to receive free food. "I remember how it feels to be treated in an impolite, degrading way," she said, "so here I'm determined to treat everyone as kindly as possible." Twenty kids, ranging from 5 to 15 years of age, worked with her. She introduced me to newly baptized members whose first contact with the Adventist Church was in her Community Services center. She could have said, "I don't know how to manage this place." Instead she offered to try. And "her did what her could."

We don't have to be a Handel and write *The Messiah* to praise the Lord with song. We don't have to have a degree in social work to love people. I believe that when we do our best at whatever needs to be done, whether we are an expert in the field or not, Jesus appreciates and blesses our efforts. And we earn Serita's compliment: "Her did what her could."

People Builders Needed

You can sing only three notes, and worse than that, you don't sing them at the right time," said the church school music teacher when I asked to sing in the school choir. So later when I entered Wisconsin Academy, I could only dream about being in the choir. Other students stood in the maroon robes with white collars . . . and sang . . . and smiled. Every year I wished that I too could sing with the group, but I didn't try out, because I didn't want to have more embarrassment.

One day, however, a surprise came. Louise Larmon, Wisconsin Academy's choir teacher, invited me to *join the choir*. I was just thrilled, but I was afraid that if she found out about my lack of ability she would kick me out. I couldn't really do anything to enhance the choir, but the choir enhanced my life. Miss Larmon was a musician, but beyond that, she was a teacher. Her business was building people, and she was helping to build me.

One day when some of the main singers in my section were sick, Miss Larmon asked me to sing a little louder. I was afraid. I wasn't sure I could hit the notes. Later she made the simple remark, "You did a good job." It's been 40 years since she said those words, but I still distinctly remember her comment. In the ministry I've often been called upon to lead music. The training that I received in her choir has been valuable to me. She made a difference in my life. She enhanced my ministry in the Adventist Church. But not mine alone.

She taught kids for 41 years at Wisconsin Academy! Can you believe it? Forty-one years of dealing with rebellious teenagers and building them into better people.

Anyone who knows about Wisconsin Academy also knows the name of Mildred Summerton. Miss Summerton was successively teacher, registrar, and principal at Wisconsin Academy during a career of 41 years in one institution. But no matter what her job description, her real job, like Miss Larmon's, was building people.

Soon after I had given my life to Jesus, I was asked to speak at the Student Week of Prayer. After my talk Miss Summerton spoke to me about it. When I reflected on the fact that she seemed to be touched by what I had said, I was amazed. That's the day that I decided to give my life to the Adventist ministry.

These two women made a difference in my life and in the lives of hundreds—no, thousands—of other young people.

I wonder. Can I help some kids around me today? The people construction business! That's the business I want to be in. How about you?

The Real Issues in
Adventist Education

D rugs are an issue in Adventist schools. Most certainly they are! And praise God they are! It may be that at some schools in our country drugs are tolerated or at the most are minimally discussed, but that is not the case at Adventist schools. There the dangers of drug use are often discussed, and drug use is rarely seen. But when it is, it is a big issue. Faculty meetings are called, counselors are called in, disciplines are meted out, and sometimes students are even asked to leave school—because in Adventist schools drugs are a big issue.

Prayer in school is another issue. Well, what I mean is, it happens all the time. It happens whenever students want to pray. It happens at the beginning of most classes—with teachers leading out. It happens in the regular chapel services, which are often worship or prayer meetings. Sometimes whole weeks are set aside for an emphasis on spiritual life and prayer.

And the teaching of evolution. Well, the only teachers who really fit in the Adventist system are those who teach creationism with conviction. That doesn't mean that evolution is not mentioned. In college my daughter, who graduated from an Adventist school, took a class in which the teacher explained the evolutionary theory, pointed out problems that evolutionists can't explain, and admitted that he, as a creationist, cannot explain everything either. However, he gave a testimony about the creative power of God and shared that he believes that Jesus made all things. The next portion of the class he then showed how to teach creationism in the classroom when the students became teachers. I believe in that kind of education.

And what about academic freedom? For the truly committed Adventist teacher, the best place to find academic freedom is in the Adventist school. That's because academic freedom means that you want to discuss the things that you are discovering in your study, including your study of the things of God. The Adventist school is a place where a teacher in any discipline can say, "Do you know what I found in my study of Scripture this morning?" Only in the Adventist school is the teacher encouraged to witness about their faith in Jesus and in the transforming power of the Holy Spirit.

What are issues in Adventist education? They are the big ones—how can we better influence our students for Jesus? How can those of us who teach be better examples of Jesus' desire for us? I like those issues. Don't you?

They Broke the Rules

Well . . . it sure looks like that to me. Actually, I support them in what they did, but *you* be the judge. We all know that one must attend classes until the end of the year and then pass the final tests to graduate, but the administrators just went ahead anyway.

You see, Steve Anderson was sick—very sick. He thought that he had won his battle with cancer and so had returned to school, hoping to finish his degree. He was a married student, serious about school. But then the cancer hit again . . . swiftly. Just two months before graduation Steve was back in bed and failing fast.

The blood tests indicated that he could not live long. That is when the president of Andrews University went with other university officers to see Steve. After a brief conversation the president presented Steve with his diploma. With a great deal of effort Steve reached his hand out from under the covers and, with a smile on his face, accepted the diploma that he had worked so hard to earn. The degree was conferred on him two months before the regularly scheduled graduation. Steve passed away a few hours later.

The university administrators went beyond the normal procedure in order to be able to reward Steve for his efforts. Some may say they broke the rules. I *like* what they did. It reminds me of what Jesus did for us. The principle was clearly stated: "The soul that sinneth, it shall die" (Ezekiel 18:20). It was clear—but when Adam sinned, Jesus went beyond the clearly enunciated statement. He said, "I will die, so that Adam and Eve and all of their descendants can have the opportunity to live forever."

Jesus didn't *have* to do it. He did it because He *wanted* to do it. Not everyone was supportive, certainly not Lucifer; but He did it anyway. He went beyond the clearly understood law that "sin leads to death." He made true the text "The wages of sin is death; but the gift of God is eternal life" (Romans 6:23).

I'm thankful for Adventist educators who know when to go beyond the normal rules. And I'm really thankful for a God who will go beyond what He has already stated in the law in order to make a way of salvation possible for me. Let's reach out to accept His offer of eternal life!

Forget World Peace . . .
Concentrate on Using Your
Own Turn Signal

I saw the slogan pasted on the bumper of a car, and it makes sense to me.

Why should I talk about world peace, meanwhile causing a traffic jam here? It's not that I'm against world peace. It is just that I believe in focusing on the things that I can do something about.

People talk to me about world peace-type issues, such as a problem in "the church" in Africa or Hungary, where I have no responsibility and little knowledge. It isn't that I have no interest, but the issue that really grabs me is "Have you led your neighbor to Jesus yet?" Now, that is a local issue that is important . . . one that you can do something about.

Sometimes a letter arrives describing everything negative about an Adventist college on the far side of the nation or some problem in a conference much too far south, east, or west to be in my sphere of influence. I can do very little to help those situations; neither do I want to get high blood pressure worrying about them. Like the slogan on the bumper, I want to concentrate on my own turn signal—do the things that *I* can do.

A few years ago I was part of a committee on the campus of Andrews University, commissioned to address how to make Andrews an even more spiritually oriented place for our students. After the meeting I thought more about the subject. Though I couldn't fix all the issues on the campus, I could start someplace . . . with myself. I called the university, obtained the names of the freshman class officers, and decided that they would be my special object of prayer on Mondays during the following month. That didn't even pretend to address all the issues, but it was something that I could do.

One Sabbath I visited an Adventist church in Salt Lake City. Our son would be spending the winter there, and I wondered how they would treat him when he came to services. I sat by myself, almost daring people to speak to me. When we divided for class, I waited for *them* to approach me. But you know, as the teacher invited each one to tell his or her name, I learned that everyone in the class was a visitor. Some were in an Adventist church for the first time. I was so embarrassed about my own lack of friendliness that I started right away to get acquainted with the visitors. My job, after all, was not to evaluate the church, but rather to do what I could to make it a better place.

I can't fix all the problems in my community or in my church, but I'm going to concentrate on what is close to me . . . what I can do. I won't talk about an unfriendly church; I'll be friendly myself. I won't talk about church problems; I'll invite Jesus to be in charge of my life so that I'm not the problem. I'll forget about world peace and concentrate on using my own turn signal.

The Spiritual Emphasis
of Physics Class

D ad, what would you think if I took physics this summer at the community college rather than going back to Pacific Union College? It would be just the one course. Then I'd be able to live at home for the summer, and would plan to go back to the Adventist college this fall," said my son, Don.

Because Don had been out of school during winter quarter, he needed to take physics during the summer. He could take it at a community college just five miles from our house, rather than staying in the dorm at an Adventist school, and it would be a lot cheaper. It was, after all, only one class, and our boy did say that he had already accepted Jesus. It seemed a reasonable thing to do, so I was giving serious consideration to this idea. He ought to be able to learn the laws of our physical world at one school just as well as at another.

Before the final decision was made, however, I decided to visit with my son. "Don," I said, "your mother and I have done the best for you that we know how to do. We so desperately want you to be in heaven. That is why we have invested in a church school education for you all these years. I believe that I would rather have you attend the Adventist school, even for this one summer class, than for you to attend the community college. But you may decide, and we will support you in your decision."

Don chose to go to the Adventist college. At the close of summer Don returned home for a few days, and we visited.

He said, "Dad, I'd like to spend Sabbath afternoon with you, going through my physics book. It is the most spiritual class I've ever taken, and I would like to talk to you about it." Right then I knew that we had gotten our money's worth for the Christian education.

He talked about the moon and the stars and their distance from the earth. He then told me that God was so big and yet interested in every person. He told me of other spiritual discussions that took place in the physics lab discussions that would have been highly unlikely at a community college.

It is not that a community college would have been bad or that the material presented would have been faulty. In my opinion, however, the physics course at the Adventist college offered an additional dimension. It helped teach my son about the God of heaven. I believe that all Adventist education is, or should be, like this.

We chose Adventist education for our children because we want them to hear people openly expressing their faith in Jesus. In Adventist schools it happens every day in physics classes, math classes, English classes, in worships, at recess, in the dormitories, and everywhere else teachers see students.

We don't send our children to Adventist schools because we think they are better at teaching reading, writing, and arithmetic. We send them for the added dimension of Christian teachers who regularly share their faith. It's for this reason that I encourage young people to consider an Adventist education. I want every young person to hear about Jesus every day.

Our church must do everything possible to tell everyone about Jesus as often as possible. Our Adventist schools are a part of this mission.

He Found Me

I did not find Jesus. In fact, I did not even go looking for Him. I didn't know about Him or realize there was a need. It would be right to say, I suppose, that I was like the lost coin of Jesus' parable. It neither knew it was lost nor sought to be found.

It was when I was a boy that Jesus came to our family. With no effort on our part to seek Him, He came looking for us. My father was in the furnace business in Merrill, Wisconsin, when he won the contract to install the new furnace in the Adventist church. Later he went to the church elder's home to bid on his furnace. Through those encounters the elder came to our home to give Bible studies. We had not known what we were missing nor how good it was to serve Jesus. Nevertheless, though we were ignorant of His love, Jesus came looking for us.

Later, during my academy years, I wandered away from Jesus. Even then, I can't say I found my way back to Jesus. Instead I was running away from Him. But again He came looking for me. I can take no credit for the fact that we got together again. My story was like the picture in the book *Pilgrim's Progress,* showing the man running away from God and God running after him with a pardon in His hand. "If you will only slow down long enough," God is calling, "I want to give you this pardon." Finally I allowed Jesus back into my life. He was right there all the time. Never was He hiding from me.

I'm so thankful that we have a God who loved us "while we were yet sinners" (Romans 5:8). He isn't sitting on a throne saying, "When you come to your senses, you can look for Me in the palace." Every day where we are—at our jobs, in our homes, in our schools, even in the taverns and theaters, wherever we go—He is there looking for us, just hoping that we will give Him a chance to enter our lives.

Even when we turn our back on Him, even when we shake our fist in His face and yell, "Leave me alone" (another definition of sin), He waits patiently to have another chance at our lives. He doesn't give up easily. After all, He gave His life for us. He went to the cross in order to gain the chance to give us eternal life.

He won't give up on us while there is any hope that we might accept His invitation to accept eternal life.

I'm so thankful for a Jesus like that. I didn't go out searching the world over for Him, putting in time and money to find an elusive God. He came looking for me, when I didn't know about Him, when I didn't even care about Him.

No, I didn't find Him; but I thank God that He found me.

Will There Be Any
Vegetarians in Heaven?

D on't answer too quickly. Think it over. Being right does not qualify a person for heaven. Some of Jesus' strongest rebukes were for people who were *right*. No question about it . . . being a vegetarian is a good idea. It does not, however, carry with it a ticket to heaven. Neither does it give one the right to cut down those who have not yet accepted the practice.

Jesus preached sermons about how we ought to act, about how we should be kind to one another. He even suggested that it would be better to die than to hurt a child. Once He said that the way to determine if a person is really one of His disciples is to see if he loves fellow church members. Kindness and thoughtfulness seemed high on His list. You know . . . stuff like visiting the people in prison, caring for the widows and fatherless, letting others get the honors. Stuff like that.

One time I met with a church board to discuss a new pastor. One of the elders was urging that they needed a conservative pastor. When it came time to do some voting, the man put in *several* ballots. It seemed odd to me that a person would think that stuffing the ballot box (a form of cheating) would be acceptable if it was being done for a good cause.

Being right does not give people a license to be cantankerous, nor does being right carry with it an obligation to keep the Sabbath school teacher right on all points.

One day my father was accosted by someone wanting to offer him some advice on his eating habits. My dad, rather ungraciously, responded by saying, "Why is it that all of you health nuts cannot keep your nose in your own business?" And I too wonder, *Why is it?* And why is it that people who are so right on theology need to correct everyone in sight? That is not witnessing! Well, actually it is, but not good witnessing. Valuable witnessing is giving a testimony about what Jesus has done for you.

Can a vegetarian go to heaven? I hope so, because I've been one for 45 years. But heaven is not available to me *because* I've been a vegetarian. Nor is it available to me because I believe in the correct Sabbath, or because I listen to the right music. Heaven is available only as a gift from Jesus, who died for all sinners—sinners with right theology, sinners with bad theology, and sinners who are vegetarians, too.

In the time before Jesus comes again, let's not be right and obnoxious. Let's all invite Jesus to live in us so we will treat others, whether they are right or wrong, as who they also are—sons and daughters of God.

Have You Been Bitten by a Mosquito Today?

Snow was flying. The roads were slick. It was shivering cold. January brings that kind of weather. But, on the up side, I took a brief, nonscientific poll of people I met, and not one had been bitten by a mosquito all day. There is *always* something for which one can be thankful.

The apostle Paul is respected as a man of God who wrote much of the New Testament, but he did not live an unruffled life. He was shipwrecked, beaten, run out of town, imprisoned, and sentenced to death. Still Paul was able to say that he'd learned to be content with whatever was happening to him. He encouraged the people in Ephesus to develop an attitude of gratitude and always give thanks to God for everything (Ephesians 5:20). King David too talked a lot about thanksgiving and praise.

I surely have many things for which to be thankful . . . things that cause me to praise God. I think today of my father, who spent the last few months of his life, as he battled cancer, sitting in his chair looking out the window. He said to me, "I have so much to be grateful for—God, the church, the people around here. Just look, here I am sick, and they even bring me food to eat. Why should I complain?"

When I was a boy, a popular song said, "When I am worried and I can't sleep, I count my blessings, instead of sheep; and I'll fall asleep counting my blessings." Right now I'm going to take just five minutes to tell God thank You.

(pause)

Wow, that five minutes went fast, and there were still a lot of things I didn't get around to mentioning. I had not even gotten to the topic of mosquitos in Michigan in January. If I get to feeling low, I think I'll go to the store and try to buy mosquito repellent in January. It will remind me that I do have things for which to be thankful.

You are at the end of this editorial now. Do you have five more minutes? Just say, "Dear Lord, may I take this opportunity to thank You for . . ."

Don't Preach That Stuff

In the early days of Adventism the Adventist Church was just opening its evangelistic work in the state of Wisconsin, and already the members were fighting! A pastor had traveled from Michigan to Wisconsin to preach to each of the small groups of believers. But every place he preached, an argument broke out over his message.

After returning to Michigan, the pastor attempted to set James White straight on the points he had put forth. Elder White could soon see that it would be easy to disagree with this pastor. He could understand why so many people in Wisconsin had become upset with the pastor's preaching. The two continued in discussion for some time. Finally James White asked, "Has anyone been saved because of your preaching that point of view?"

"No," the pastor admitted.

"Well, then," Elder White said, "don't preach that stuff anymore."

Often people have tried to involve me in a discussion of the finer points of theology, but I have wanted to ask, "Has anyone been saved because of that stuff?" And with James White I say, "Well, if not, why preach it?"

Some like to spend a lot of time discussing such topics as the nature of Christ and can easily force a listener into a *for* or *against* position. However, it seems to me that the discussion of the power of Jesus to overcome sin is the message that touches people's hearts and leads them to accept Him as their personal Saviour.

I do enjoy a good argument now and then, but never have I seen anyone saved because of it. When I was first in the ministry, a flyer came to our home discussing the teachings of a church in our city. I sat right down at my typewriter and typed a lengthy reply, arguing about many of the points in the article. My wife said, "Surely you are not going to send that, are you?" Of course I was! I had every intention of sending it, and the points that I made were absolutely correct, but it hasn't been sent yet. No one would have been saved because of that kind of arguing.

I think that before I go too long on *any* subject, I'm going to apply the James White test. If I cannot answer that someone has been saved by the preaching of that message, then I think I will reserve that topic for discussion during the millennium. I'll go back to the tried and true message of Jesus—His love for sinners and His ability to forgive. Like Paul, I determine "not to know anything among you, save Jesus Christ, and him crucified" (1 Corinthians 2:2). Then I know I'll be talking about something that results in the salvation of sinners. That message got me . . . and it will get others, too.

Keep It Simple

"What would I have to do to be an Adventist?" the piano teacher asked our 12-year-old son.

"Well," he responded, "mostly what you need to do is to love Jesus."

I've thought about it and haven't come up with a better answer. It was pretty simple; but then, Jesus spoke of eternal things in very simple ways too.

When the lawyer was ready to turn the law into an all-day debate, he asked Jesus which of the commandments were really the most important. Jesus summarized the matter with a few simple words: Love God, and love people.

In the Old Testament, too, there is a description of what the Lord requires. If we want to please Him, should we give big offerings—thousands of calves or rams or rivers of oil—or should we bow down or give our children? No, that isn't it. The answer is in Micah 6:8. If you want to please God, live by these three principles: "Do justly," "Love mercy," and "Walk humbly with thy God."

Do you wonder about your own religion, if you have the right kind? There is a text for that, too. "Pure religion . . . is this, To visit the fatherless and widows . . . and to keep . . . unspotted from the world" (James 1:27). This is simply put—no commentaries are needed to understand it.

In some ways it's easier to discuss original sin or the nature of Christ.

Arguing such difficult topics doesn't require conclusions or life changes. But the simple statements in the paragraphs above are direct, to the point, and hard to get around. They require a specific lifestyle.

So do you want to know how things will go at the judgment at the end of the world? Jesus gave us a "review sheet" of what would be on the final test. It is not complicated either. It is very easy to understand. As the old spiritual says, "Everybody talkin' 'bout heaven ain't goin' there." Jesus said He will say to some, "Come into My kingdom, because you are the ones who took food to the hungry, gave something to drink to those who were thirsty, received strangers, attended sick people, helped the poor, and visited people in prison" (see Matthew 25).

A simple question with far-reaching implications is: What difference is my love for Jesus making in the way I live? Am I inviting Him to motivate and empower me to do justly, to love people, to visit the sick, the poor, and those in prison? If it is not doing all that, maybe I am only like sounding brass or a tinkling cymbal.

If I am not, the answer to the problem is easy: Simply give Jesus permission every day to live His love in you, in everything you do and everything you say.

Dear Jesus, help me to love You so much that You really make a difference in my life.

Preaching About the Devil

I'd preach about the devil," he said.

Several people had recommended this man as a good camp meeting speaker, so I called him. And I asked him, "What is your favorite topic?"

"The devil," he replied. "I have a whole series about the devil. I could preach every day of the weeklong camp meeting about the devil."

I did not invite him. In fact, I told him that we couldn't use him as a speaker at our camp meeting. "We already know about the devil," I told him. "Too many of us have had too much personal experience with him already. What we need to know is more about Jesus. We need to hear about His power."

Sometimes people give me a list of things about which to preach: Call sin by its right name! Preach on standards or health reform or . . . You know what I mean. While all of these should receive some of our attention, what I really need to know is "Can Jesus change my life?" People in our churches can benefit by knowing that Jesus can save troubled marriages; He can give the victory over bad habits; He can forgive sin. He is the answer to our needs.

Recently my son told me, "There are a lot of churches in my area, but I usually go to the one where the pastor will likely be talking about Jesus. That is what I need in my experience right now."

That is what we all need! In our churches, our Sabbath

school classes, and our personal visits, let's let people hear more, not about sin or the originator of sin, but more about Jesus.

How to Practice Medicine Without a Degree

This is not about getting rid of doctors or hospitals, but it is about dispensing some very potent medicine. You don't have to be a graduate of any medical school to use this medicine. And you can use it for yourself or for other people.

Although many medical books do not even mention this treatment, an increasing number of studies have been done, and articles that clearly demonstrate the positive results have been published in scientific journals. Researchers from Georgetown, Duke, and Harvard met with representatives of the National Institutes of Health and the National Institute for Healthcare Research to "stimulate an explosion of research in religion in health." The effect of prayer in medical treatment was one of the issues being studied.

Prayer for the sick can be described in one of the following ways: (1) of no value, (2) a negative value, or (3) a positive value. There is only one right answer. And research is proving what we have known all along—prayer is a positive value. In the Randolph Byrd study of people being treated for heart problems in San Francisco General Hospital, those prayed for had "less congestive heart failure during recovery, had to use fewer diuretics, were less frequently intubated and experienced fewer cases of pneumonia and cardiopulmonary arrests" than those in the control group, for whom the intercessors had not prayed. Other studies too show quicker and more complete recoveries among people who are the subject of prayer.

The only thing really surprising about all of this is that we pray so little.

This week I was visiting in a home when the home-health nurse arrived. After asking several medical questions, she said to the patient, "Before I came, I was thinking about you and preparing for this visit. I brought the texts with me that I have picked out for you." After reading the Bible texts, she prayed. The patient was moved and greatly appreciated the visit.

I'm not a medical professional, but I can administer such treatments. God offers to hear and answer prayer, so my part is to visit the sick and pray for them. This can only enhance the other medical treatment they are receiving.

At this moment I can think of several people who need this powerful medicine. Some are sick, some discouraged, some trying to make a decision. I am giving them doses right now. I am praying for them. God will not turn a deaf ear to my prayers. He promised to listen, and I know He will.

There is no prescription needed for this medicine. I am going to administer it daily, even several times a day. How about you?

Where Were You
This Past Sabbath?

Where were *you* last Sabbath morning? Oh, I'm not asking which church you attended, or even *if* you attended. I am asking, Where was your head? About what were you thinking, and how did you relate to what was taking place during the worship service?

Usually at church on Sabbath morning we have music, prayer, and spoken words. Where were you while this was happening?

Some people looked as though they were in church worshiping, but actually they were busy serving as judges—kind of like the judges at the Olympics. They sat in church, all right, but after the music or the sermon they thought, *I'd give that a 5.7.* They judged it in competition with other music or sermons.

Others went to a fashion show. Their body was at church, but they saw what people were wearing and might even have been a bit upset about skirt lengths or hairstyles. When they left for church they gave themselves the once-over in the full-length mirror and wondered, *How do I look? What will people think?*

Others in the same church were concerned about the music—too loud, too fast, too sharp, or too flat.

If you were one of those who were taking part last Sabbath, where were you? Were you on stage giving your best performance, and surely hoped that people liked it? Were you giving an oration?

A woman asked Jesus in John 4:20 where we should worship, but Jesus turned the answer in a direction she did not expect. It is not *where* we worship, but that we truly *worship* God that is important.

This coming Sabbath when I go to church, I do not want to be at a fashion show, in the critics' corner, or in the gallery watching a show. My prayer will be "Lord, I know that I have done nothing to deserve to be in Your presence. Please forgive my sins, and let my worship be acceptable in Thy sight." And I will seek to truly worship—as we sing and pray and listen to the Scripture and the minister's message, I'll give an offering and pray, "Dear Jesus, bless this offering, and please take me and my talents as a part of this offering."

This Sabbath I don't want merely to attend church. This Sabbath I will be in the presence of my God, and I will worship Him.

You Don't Criticize a Bride

The comment heard most often at a wedding is "Isn't she a beautiful bride!" Although brides come in a variety of sizes, shapes, and colors, we still hear the comment "She really makes a beautiful bride." Criticizing the bride just *isn't* the thing to do.

Sometimes the bride arrives late for the wedding; yet the guests wait patiently and smile approvingly as she comes up the aisle. At times, after the brief ceremony in the church, a bride can be seen slipping out of her brand-new shoes and walking around in stocking feet at the reception, but no one makes a big deal out of it. And why do people stand in a long line? To offer criticism, constructive or otherwise? No! It is to greet the smiling bride.

Just for a moment, imagine with me a wedding guest saying, "I used to teach that girl in school. Back then she had a terrible problem with acne. I'm wondering if she has gotten over the problem yet. I'm sitting too far back to see well, but I've heard a rumor that she has a big red pimple on her neck that her dress does not cover when she moves in certain ways. Could someone up closer tell me if it is there? I have a right to know. After all, I was her teacher. She needs to be open about such things."

Now, isn't that preposterous! We don't go to the wedding to look for flaws. No! We are all delighted that the girl who yesterday was in ragged jeans, dirty tennis shoes, and a faded school sweatshirt is now this beautiful bride.

Often the church is referred to as the bride of Jesus (Ephesians 5:25-27; Revelation 19:7, 8), and there is no object on earth that receives as much of His love as does His church. Jesus is in the business of taking people of all different sizes and shapes and colors, who have all kinds of scars and pimples, and making of them a beautiful church—His bride. Everybody doesn't look all that perfect just yet. In fact, some still seem to have a bad case of acne. But I don't want to criticize the bride, because I've never met a bridegroom who appreciated someone's finding defects in his bride. Neither have I read a Bible text about great joy in heaven when someone is first to spot something wrong with the church or one of its leaders. No credit is given to the one who is first to publish that on paper or on the Internet.

Knowing that Jesus is so madly in love with His bride encourages me to be bold in saying, "I'm in love with His church too." At times she may seem to be a bit feeble or even to look as though she may fall, but I'm planning to stay close to her. I believe God when He says that the church will be special to Him until the day that Jesus comes again.

Jesus, thank You for the great love You have for Your church. I am sorry for the times that I have talked bad about Your chosen bride. And Jesus, because she is in love with You, isn't she a beautiful bride? . . . and growing lovelier by the day!

Speak Positively

H ush! Don't say a word if you can't say something good!" Do you remember that admonition from Mom? I want to second her rule. Please don't say anything discouraging to others in the church. If you are tempted to speak negatively, beg God to protect you from doing so.

God cares about your attitudes and expressions toward His work. A law of battle in Old Testament times was that one who was afraid was to return home rather than join in the fray. In fact, anyone who had recently built a house, planted a vineyard, or become engaged to be married was also sent home. God wanted soldiers whose hearts would be in the work at hand. Those who were afraid might be tempted to tell their companions that the project was too big, or that too many were fighting for the enemy, thus discouraging those who had the faith to believe the goal *could* be accomplished (Deuteronomy 20:5-8). God did not want these naysayers in His army.

The challenges we as a church face today are great too. There are millions who don't know Jesus. When someone has a bold idea of a way to spread the gospel, it is easy for someone to say "It won't work." Even though some voiced their doubt when we were preparing for NET '95, more than 600 churches participated, and more than 5,000 people were baptized.

Consider what the Lord has done through NET evangelism since!

It is easy to think of reasons that church initiatives will not work—perhaps the greatest being that we ourselves won't work. It is harder, but definitely more rewarding, to help God make them work.

God told Gideon and others about to go to war to send the fainthearted home. I don't want to be kicked out of God's army. I don't want to discourage other loyal soldiers. Today I'm praying, "Dear Father, please don't let me say anything that would discourage *anyone* from working for You. Help me to be an encourager today. I don't want to be fainthearted . . . I want to dream, plan, and do big things in Your name."

It's Just a Big Numbers Game, Isn't It?

It has been said more than once. It really makes me sad, but I have heard it. "Is it just a big numbers game?" It's been said about Sabbath school attendance, tithe records, even baptisms after an evangelistic meeting.

Jesus was into numbers. Just look at some of the stories He told. He talked about the woman who had lost one of her 10 coins. If she had not been counting, she never would have known that one was missing. And there is that story about the one lost sheep. Ninety-nine were in the fold; one was missing. Now, when you are surrounded by 99 sheep, you don't just happen to know that one is missing. You would have to be counting.

We were praying for 600 baptisms in the conference when I was president of the New Jersey Conference. We had almost reached that number when there was an evangelistic meeting in our home church. As evangelist Lynn Martell made the call and our son stepped forward requesting baptism, I did not say, "That's number 596." He was not just a number. It hurts me to think that he *could be* just a number. He is our only son, and yet he *was* one of the 600 to be baptized. You know what? Every one is someone's son or daughter. And every *one* is a child of God. No one is just a number.

Every Sabbath, in every church, we could count every person just to make sure there are none missing. When I was the pastor of a church, we took a vacation, and our Sabbath school teacher wrote us a note saying that we had been missed. It felt good! We would really cut down on our problem of missing members if all missing persons would receive a note from church members the first time they skipped services, even if we already knew why they were missing.

As long as there are lost people out there, we should be interested in quantity as well as quality. Numbers are important, especially when they represent people Jesus died to redeem. Let's count them in Sabbath school and count them in church. Let's rejoice over every *one* of them—and really rejoice when there are more sinners present—and let's go looking for any who are missing.

Is There a Home Field Advantage in the Adventist Church?

W hat we need are more people who will call sin by its right name."

I've heard that statement dozens of times. And I'm sure it is true. We could use more people calling sin by its right name, particularly if each person is looking at his own life, into her own heart. But another great need is for a lot more people who can recognize good deeds of others, see their positive actions, and be willing to speak about them, too.

Many people around us are really in fragile emotional condition. For them, a sincere compliment would be wonderful medicine and would even encourage them to continue doing good deeds.

I once heard my mother say, "I have no talents. The best that I can do is to encourage others." I've seen her encourage juniors at Sabbath school with words about their participation in Sabbath school or church. They are better kids because of that visit.

There are many teachers who have not heard a positive word from parents or constituents for a long time. When bad things happen around school, many of us feel compelled to speak to school staff about what is going wrong. But is it not also good to speak to them about the good things that are happening? Let's go to the school just looking for good things, make a list of everything good that we find, and write a letter to everyone connected to the school telling them of our findings.

How about the preacher, the church secretary, or some other person in church work. There is a good chance that many people notice their mistakes and have already pointed them out. There is an equally good chance that few have noticed or commented on the regular good work done. While I was a conference president, I received many letters telling me about mistakes of pastors, but I did not average even one letter a year telling me about good things pastors had done.

Sports teams like to play in their own hometown. The actual basketball court is the same size, and the hoop is always regulation distance from the floor. The difference is the crowd. The great home court advantage is that their fans are rooting for them. They cheer the players and give them the benefit of the doubt on close calls. In a baseball game fans seated hundreds of feet away from home plate can call strikes and balls to the advantage of the home team and are even willing to yell at an umpire who does not see it the same way they do.

Let's give those around us the advantage of being the home team. If we cheer on the pastors and teachers in our area, they will become even better workers. Of course, they will not make a home run every time. They might even strike out once in a while. They know it too. But they can recover more quickly when we focus on the good they are doing.

Join me in complimenting *someone* today. They will be better for it, and so will you.

A Lot of the Bible Sounds Crazy

It sounds crazy to say that a 90-year-old woman will have a baby or that an already-buried dead man is only sleeping. We'd call an army general who came up with the idea of walking around a city as the strategy for its defeat crazy. And it would really seem crazy to try to feed 5,000 people with a kid's lunch. We could expect to find these stories in *Ripley's Believe It or Not* perhaps.

But it is all true. Sarah and Abraham did have the baby, just as Jesus promised. Although he was dead and buried, Lazarus came out of the grave alive at Jesus' call. When Joshua followed the Lord's instructions, he was able to capture Jericho. Never mind that it didn't *sound* like a good strategic plan. And when Jesus asked for the kid's lunch, although it sounded crazy the 5,000 were fed.

Some other stories are even more difficult to believe. For instance, that a person can be forgiven again for the very same thing, even though they were just forgiven *only days or hours or even minutes before,* sounds crazy. But it is true! Jesus really does that.

Another thing that *sounds* crazy is the judgment. The judgment is not at all about how much good a person has done weighed against how much bad he or she has done. It is all about letting Jesus take our place in the judgment. Then the bad, the sin, is just dumped into the bottom of the ocean. Jesus says, "Don't look at those sins. Look at My record, not his, not hers." This judgment is not like any judgment you have ever heard of before.

It does sound crazy, too, to think that a person who has been sinning and who asks forgiveness is forgiven—no questions asked, even if it is murder, stealing, lying, pride . . . anything. But it is true. Jesus forgives! Then follows the almost unbelievable thought, "There is therefore now no condemnation to them which are in Christ Jesus" (Romans 8:1). A most reverent "Wow!" escapes my lips. Do I understand it? No, I don't. But do I believe it? Yes! And I praise God for it and thank Him for salvation, for forgiveness.

The craziest thought of all, however, is that Jesus would be interested enough in me to forgive me and to come back to get me. But it is true. And He is *interested* in you.

Are you sometimes tempted to doubt God's ability or His loving desire to forgive—to save you? Do you wonder if it is really true? Read again God's own words offering forgiveness and salvation, "For God so loved the world, that he gave his only begotten Son, that whosoever believeth in him should not perish, but have everlasting life" (John 3:16). Believe them and claim them as His promise to you.

This Is Not
as Good as It Gets

E njoy it . . . this is about as good as it gets." *The Kiplinger Letter* said it. Jobs and income growing, reasonable interest rates, low inflation . . . It's a happy set of circumstances, so let's enjoy it. The newsletter continued to talk about robust exports, sky-high consumer confidence, and a jack-in-the-beanstalk stock market. And, the newsletter advised, it will go on for a while.

Sorry, Mr. Kiplinger, but you just don't understand. It does get better than this—a lot better! You should have been with me at worship this morning in our office. We prayed for a man who is struggling with cancer, who may need a bone marrow transplant. Try telling him that it doesn't get better than this. We prayed for a woman whose baby was sick. We prayed for a family whose child had just died and another whose father had died. I am so pleased to be able to tell you that *The Kiplinger Letter* is wrong. It does get better than this!

To those living in a country where religious freedom does not exist, it does get better than this. To Don junior, our son doing a medical-school rotation in Papua New Guinea, it does get better. Someday your skills won't be needed to fix sick and injured people.

To those like my mother- and father-in-law who lived in the retirement estates, who had difficulty hearing and seeing, the good news is that it does get better than this.

And while I'm sending personal messages, here is one for you, Dad, while you live alone missing Mom since her death a few months ago, and for others in similar circumstances: I can tell you with conviction, don't worry. Mr. Kiplinger was wrong! Perhaps he is right in that it may not get any better *here,* but the good news is, it does get better.

A great day is coming soon. Just picture it . . . Jesus coming! Graves opening! The sick becoming well! The stock market mattering no more! Yes! Kiplinger is wrong. It does get better. It will get better. And it will be soon. Praise the name of Jesus.

It Ain't Over

Winston Churchill walked to the podium to give the commencement address. It was right during the discouraging part of World War II. He looked to one side of the audience and said, "Never give up." He looked toward the middle of the audience and said, "Never give up." He turned to the other side of the audience and said, "Never give up." Then he sat down. His message was clear and has not been forgotten.

Yogi Berra, the famous catcher for the New York Yankees, expressed the same sentiment when he said, "It ain't over till it's over."

If you feel discouraged today as you pray for your husband or wife, son or daughter, father or mother, neighbor . . . or whomever . . . *don't give up*. If things don't seem to be going well, if they don't seem to have any interest in spiritual things, I want to remind you that it's not over yet.

The Bible is full of stories that show how God works with people long after we might be tempted to give up. Samson disappointed his parents and his God often, but God didn't give up on him. In fact, Samson can be found in the Hebrews 11 lineup of God's special people. And the woman at Jacob's well . . . and even Peter . . . would we have despaired over them?

Ellen White implied that there is hope for every person when she wrote, "A desire for goodness . . . exists in every heart" (*Education,* p. 29). In *Evangelism* she declared, "None have fallen so low, . . . but that they can find deliverance in Christ" (p. 626).

I encourage you to stay close to Jesus—in His Word and in prayer—and never give up on inviting others to come to Him. If you yourself have not asked Him to come into your life lately, I want to tell you that it is not too late to recommit your life to Him. Once again I am giving myself to Jesus . . . at this very moment; and I invite you to do the same.

I agree with Yogi Berra that "it's not over till it's over." I tell you, it is not over. Many will give themselves to Jesus yet. Keep praying for that friend or relative. Jesus is still calling to them. Never give up. Never!

We Are Rich!

I'm rich. You might be surprised to hear me say that, but it really is true. I've been taking inventory and have come to realize how really rich I am. However, you might not even be able to recognize it by my lifestyle. Let me explain.

Once I attended a board meeting of Christian Record Services. This Seventh-day Adventist organization ministers to those who are deaf and who are blind. When it came time to vote on the board, we were asked to vote by voice and by raising our hands at the same time. This would allow the deaf board members to see the voting as it proceeded and all the blind board members to hear the votes being cast. Each time we voted I was reminded of how wonderful it is to see and to hear.

I am a rich man. I have eyes that see, and I have ears that hear.

A few years ago my wife and I spent a month in the country of Estonia, conducting evangelistic meetings. Our group, plus 10 other people, stayed in a dormitory. At first I thought, *We'll never eat here—the kitchen is too dirty.*

Later, as we became better acquainted in the city, we were so thankful that we had our own kitchen facilities where we could boil water before cooking or drinking. There was no place in the entire city where we felt it would be healthy to get a drink of water. Many countries in our world do not have clean water. In the United States we can leave our homes and go anywhere to get a drink of water anytime we wish.

I am a rich man. I have water to drink—all the water I

want, anytime I want it.

In Estonia we could not find clean restrooms. Our dorm bathrooms were neither clean nor private. Upon first viewing them, I thought that I would wait until I went downtown and would use the restrooms there. But one trip downtown convinced me that I would wait until I got back to the dormitory. When I returned to the United States, I drove past gas stations with clean bathrooms and saw rest areas along the highway with nice bathrooms. Suddenly I realized that restrooms were available everywhere in the United States. I stood in a bathroom, looked around, and prayed, "Thank You, Lord, for such a beautiful bathroom."

I am a rich man. There is a bathroom wherever I need one.

While visiting the Romanian Seventh-day Adventist Church in Chicago, I realized that many of the members had risked their lives to be able to experience freedom. I was told an amusing story about two dogs who met each other while trying to escape their oppressive country. One dog supposedly asked the other dog, "Why do you want to leave?" The other dog replied, "Just so I can bark when I want to."

I am a rich man. I have freedom. I can have opinions that are different from the opinions held by those around me, and I can express those opinions too.

But best of all, I have been offered eternal life. And it's free! Jesus wants to give life to everyone; I have accepted His gift.

I am a rich man! Please accept the gift He offers. You will be rich too.

Don't Play It Safe—
Take Risks

Get out of the rut! Do things differently! Be bold! The New Testament says that Peter and his friends turned the world upside down. Some thought they were drunk. That reputation didn't come from wearing both suspenders and a belt—they took risks.

There always will be plenty of people telling you why something can't be done. There always will be people telling you to play it safe. But I say, "Go for it!"

What about planting a new church in your town? Some will say, "It can't be done!" But why not ask God if He would like to have it done? Maybe He is looking to increase His market share over the devil and would like to do it with another church in your city.

You have never conducted an evangelistic meeting? Well, you can't start any younger! Do it in your church or at a local motel or in your own home. Hundreds of young people have run hundreds of Revelation seminars. That worked too, and hundreds of people have been baptized as a result. Those young people didn't have enough experience to know that it couldn't be done. They followed the simple directions outlined in the director's kit, and God blessed.

You've never been outside the United States? Why not join a Maranatha trip and help build a new church in the Dominican Republic, for instance? Link up with fellow church members or get community members to join you. Now . . . how do you know they won't go? Several friends of Adventists have already gone. Some non–Seventh-day Adventist Christians have been thrilled to have a part in building a church.

Let's press ourselves to go beyond our usual boundaries. Let's ask more people to accept Jesus. I too have been afraid of offending people, so at times I've not witnessed as openly as I wish I had. It's time to take greater risks. The chances of offending someone with our witness is not as great a possibility as being too quiet in our witness. When I think about how many people I've offended by asking them to accept Jesus, I realize that the list is not nearly as long as the list of those I've never asked at all.

One pastor I know regularly asks people, "What would it take for you to accept Jesus?" No one gets mad. Nobody dies of a heart attack. This pastor leads more people to Jesus than almost anyone I know. I want to be more bold too.

Time is short. Radio and TV move from one commercial to another in 15 or 30 seconds. A long commercial is one minute. And a really long infomercial is a half hour. Subjects change often. Why do I think I must wait for just the right time to say something for Jesus?

I think I'll take more risks for God, attempt bigger things for Him. My new prayer will be "Lord, forgive me for my timid ways, my small plans, my fears. Cover my mistakes in the future, and help me to be fearless for You. Let me do more for You. Help me to do even things that I've never done before. And help me to mean it when I say to You, 'You are looking for someone? Well, here I am. You can send me!' "

Stamp Out
Stinkin' Thinkin'

Stinkin' thinkin' and good preachin' don't mix well. On Sabbath morning I don't want stinkin' thinkin' going on in my head. I cannot allow negative thoughts to take over. Critical thoughts must be driven out. You see, on Sabbath morning I am preparing to preach.

There is a lot for me to do on a Sabbath morning when I am going to preach. When I get up in the morning, I'm thinking about the sermon. And when I'm getting ready for church, I'm going over the sermon. I try to be very careful about what I eat to make sure that my body is ready to preach. But even more important, I must be careful about what is in my mind. If I am driving for an hour or two to the church, I visit a little with my wife, but only about certain topics. You see, I can't afford to have a topic brought up that might cause me to feel negative or critical. Mostly I just review my sermon in my mind and spend the rest of the time praying.

After I arrive at church, I greet the people. But I'm still thinking about my sermon, and praying. If someone does a really lousy job on their part in Sabbath school, I can't afford to think about it. If I see someone who is dressed in a way that seems inappropriate for church, I try not to notice. But if I do see it, I have to erase it from my mind as quickly as possible. I don't want anyone in the church to discuss other members with me. I don't want to hear anything bad about a church elder or the pastor or any person.

You see, I am getting ready to speak to the people about

and for Jesus. I can't afford to be diverted into negative or critical thoughts. No stinkin' thinkin'—none!

But now the thought comes to me: *What if I were to live my whole life that way? What if I never gave any time to negative thoughts? What if I never criticized anyone or listened to anyone who wanted to criticize others? What if I never spent any time with stinkin' thinkin'? What if I always had my brain and my attitude in the position of being ready to talk to people about Jesus?*

Maybe this is what Paul had in mind when he said, "Whatsoever things are true, whatsoever things are honest, whatsoever things are just . . . whatsoever things are lovely, whatsoever things are of good report; if there be any virtue, and if there be any praise, think on these things" (Philippians 4:8).

I'd like to spend a whole day like that. Well, why not? Even a week, a month, thinking only about good things.

Dear Jesus, please stamp out stinkin' thinkin' from my mind and let me think on true, honest, lovely things. Help me to think no critical thoughts, but give me thoughts of praise. Thank You, Jesus!

Been Here Long Enough—
Time to Move On

It has been good. Things have gone well. A certain predictability has set in. And that makes any of us feel more comfortable. No, I am not complaining about things, but it *is* time to move on. I don't want to stay in the same place forever—not even for a decade. Well, for that matter, not even a year . . . or even a day. It's time to move on.

When the Puritans left for America, their pastor, who stayed behind, stood by the boat and challenged them to keep moving. It is easy to fall into a routine, to coast along without giving real thought to what is happening. It is so easy to do just what we did yesterday, which is a repeat of last week. Don't stop in your Christian walk where you are today.

My father loved the song "I'm pressing on the upward way, new heights I'm gaining every day; still praying as I onward bound, 'Lord, plant my feet on higher ground.'" That's what I want. That's it exactly! I want to keep pressing on to higher ground. I want to be closer to Jesus today than I was yesterday, and closer yet tomorrow than I am today.

Couples often renew their commitments to each other, and as they do, their relationship grows. That's what I have in mind. Here and now I am renewing my commitment to Jesus—evaluating the amount of time that I've been spending with Him, the time we've been talking to each other, and the gifts that I've been giving Him. I'm not planning to live on a plateau.

When our family first became Adventists, things *really*

changed. On that one day the language cleaned up, the tobacco was gone, the alcohol was gone, and even the meat was gone. It was a dramatic change, but I don't want to make my home on that plateau. I really like the thought that the longer I serve Jesus, the closer our friendship is and the more I enjoy being with Him. Years ago I couldn't understand how anyone could spend more than a few minutes praying. Now sometimes when I leave on a trip, I decide that it will be a time to talk more with Jesus. He rides along, and we spend the day together.

I'm happy to have a relationship with Jesus, and it's getting better by the day. Stop here? No way! That's not my plan. My plan is that every day will be a new day with Him in which I will get to know Him better.

Please join me! Let's move on to a better relationship with Jesus. Won't you make that commitment to Him right now?

Ask 'Em

"How are you able to report so many baptisms?" I asked Loren Nelson as he was working in the New York Conference. "You are always able to tell more stories of people accepting Jesus than other pastors around you. What are you doing that is different?"

What he told me seemed so obvious when I thought about it. It was the same advice that I was given when I was selling for the Fuller Brush Company, the same advice that I heard while I was selling books as a literature evangelist.

It is the same thing that Ellen White wrote in an often-quoted paragraph. But even though I had read the paragraph dozens of times, I had hardly noticed it. The emphasis is most often on the first phrases of the paragraph. We almost catch our breath when she says, "*Christ's method alone* will give true success" when it comes to winning people to Him. We are advised to mingle with people and make friends with them, simply paying attention to their goals and helping them to succeed in what is important to them (*The Ministry of Healing,* p. 143; italics supplied).

Churches that have not baptized anyone recently have difficulty finding individuals for baptism because they do not have friends outside the church circle. I can't say that I've done so well in this, either. The thought challenges me—I need to mingle with people in the community.

But the last phrase of that paragraph is just as important as the first. The phrase that really caught my attention, which is the advice given me by Loren Nelson, literature evangelists,

Fuller Brush, and Zig Zigler, is pretty simple: "Ask them!" It's as simple as that—just ask them.

After Jesus became friends with the people, and after He had gained their confidence, He said, "Come and follow Me." It's hard to sell anything—books or Fuller Brush products or Jesus, for that matter—unless you call for the order. Jesus did it by inviting, "Come and follow Me."

Sometimes we squirm a little when we hear evangelists making a *call* for accepting Jesus or the Sabbath or baptism or church membership. But that is exactly what we *all* need to do: Ask 'em!

Ask 'em to come to church. Ask 'em to accept Jesus. After you have gained their confidence, ask 'em. Do you doubt that the reason Loren Nelson led so many people to Jesus was that he asked so many people to accept Jesus? Sure, some turned him down, but because he asked so often, he had many positive responses.

How can I do that? I'm asking God that very question! Ellen White said that if I will follow Jesus' method—spend time with people, care about their needs, then ask 'em—I can find success in bringing people to Jesus. And I believe that the more I ask, the more there will be who accept.

Fuller Brush salesmen, literature evangelists . . . Move over! You don't have a corner on the market!

Baptist Minister Accuses Adventists of Misappropriating Funds

R ight off, I wondered what right he had to accuse the Adventist Church of misappropriating funds. All the money the church receives is carefully audited and disbursed only by committee action. Full reports are given regularly to church boards, or to conference, union, or General Conference committees.

He was not an antagonist looking for a fight. He seemed to be a real Christian, and he was speaking at the Adventist seminary. I heard him myself, so I know that he really said it. The speaker was Robert Logan,★ who teaches church planting all over the world. What he said was "You Adventists are really to be admired for the large amount of money you give to your church. I have to give you an 'A' on income. But I can't give you that kind of grade on how you spend your money. You spend so much on pastoring your churches and on the other activities for your own church members. You need to evaluate how much money you spend trying to reach people who have no church home at all, people who do not know Jesus."

Logan was really plain about it. He said we were not appropriating enough money for reaching lost people. Then he hammered the point home by saying, "People who are really in love with God will find their heart breaking about what breaks the heart of God. And what breaks the heart of God is that people don't know Jesus."

I really want to say that the Baptist preacher doesn't know

what he is talking about. Does he know about our mission program, or our extensive evangelistic outreaches by satellite, or otherwise? But then I did some thinking. Most of the requests for money that come to the offices of our conference and union administrators are for more pastors to care for our congregations, or for building projects for our congregations, or for some other thing for our existing churches. Very few requests have come with the appeal "We want to reach people in our community who don't know Jesus."

The preacher might be right. Even more, we might be misappropriating our time, too. How much of your time and mine is used for people who haven't found Jesus? I don't even know very many people like that. Most of my life is spent working with church members.

There is a mission field at our doorstep. Every day we see people. Before going into the grocery store, have you ever prayed "Dear Lord, if this store clerk does not know You, help me to have the right conversation with her"? What about the person at the gas station or at the post office?

I am determined to think about how I spend my time and my offerings. In fact, dear Lord, help me to appropriate my money and time wisely. And please use me today to speak to someone who doesn't know You.

---

*Robert Logan, D.Min., is the executive director of CoachNet and the president of Strategic Ministries, Inc.

Let's Clean Up
Our Church Books!

Yes! Let's clean up our church books. Let's deal with members who aren't really members anymore. I'm in favor of dropping people from church membership and other forms of church discipline. However, there are appropriate steps to take as we get ready to administer church discipline, whether it be censuring or dropping someone. Let's make sure we do it correctly.

When we first start talking about administering discipline to a member, let's turn to the head of the Love-'Em-Back committee. You do have one in your church, don't you? If not, this is the place to start. Before we talk about all the bad things that Sinful Sam and Gertie Gossip have done, we need to have a person appointed who will be in charge of loving them back. Anyone in the church can be appointed to this office. Hopefully, several will volunteer—even vie—for the position. Actually, there should be a number of committee chiefs: one for every candidate for discipline.

The chairperson will beg God to give them a burden for Sinful Sam—the kind of burden that Moses had when he told God, "If You can't forgive these people, then blot my name out of the book too." Once the chairperson feels that they would give their life for Sinful Sam, if that's what it would take to reclaim him (a precedent has been established here), they can begin to function.

The next step is to get a group of folks praying for Sinful Sam. No, no! I didn't say criticizing him—not even *constructively* criticizing him. The group will come together to pray,

and they will pray separately throughout the day. In fact, someone will be praying for Sam all day long.

Committee number two is formed next. This group needs
to be made up of seven individuals, one for each day of the
week. Sinful Sam often sins *big* on Sunday. So Right-Living
Rob makes contact with him on Sunday. They pray together,
the families go out to eat together, the guys go fishing together
or work on cars together.

On Monday Committed Carl goes by Sinful Sam's place of
work, just to encourage him. Dedicated Dan has been praying
since the previous Tuesday about what kind of contact he will
make with Sinful Sam this Tuesday.

Sabbaths have not been good at all for Sinful Sam. He hates to
go to church, because some of the members (who haven't sinned
all week) gripe at him or whisper when he passes. The whole
prayer-band team will have to help guard him from those who
think they will be translated at any moment. Every Sabbath Sam
and his family will have a dinner invitation. In fact, they will need
to be booked several weeks in advance. (One really risky thing
that Jesus tried was taking church visitors to sinners' houses to eat.
This could be bad for your reputation. They *talked* about Jesus for
doing it. It is a great way to make friends, though.)

We need to help Sinful Sam's wife, too. She's so loaded
with guilt because of the way Sam's been acting that she's
likely to come down pretty hard on him. Get the same two
committees working for her that are working for Sam.

Sam's kids need help too. They act a lot like Sam. (Don't
remind them of that, though.)

If, after a year or so of the committee's operating, Sam just
keeps on publicly embarrassing the church, then his Love-'Em-
Back chairperson needs to visit him to explain that he will need
to recommend that the church censure Sinful Sam. By this
time he and Sam will have become really good friends. If the

church *does* take the action, the committee will work harder than ever. If the Love-'Em-Back committees have not followed through, Sam's Love-'Em-Back chairperson will beg for mercy for themself and the committee, asking for more time to work for Sinful Sam.

My advice to you: Don't be too disappointed if you can't find a *good* reason to drop Sam by the end of the year. He may repent! Jonah had that problem—the whole city of Nineveh came back to God.

This sure is a lot of work to put into dropping someone like Sinful Sam. It might not be worth it, either. But Sam is *such* an important fellow. In fact, Sam is loved so much that one Man I know gave His life for him.

I'm in favor of cleaning up our church books. I hope all our churches in North America get at it right away.

I'm Writing
My Obituary Today

Today I'm writing my obituary. I worked on it yesterday—and last week. I plan to edit it a bit tomorrow, too. I'm preparing it to be read by a lot of people. Possibly it will be read at my funeral, although I'm not sure exactly when that will be. I certainly don't plan for that event to come any time soon, but when it does, someone will surely read some kind of obituary. I want it to be a good one, and I'd like to have some input on what it says.

An obituary is like a summary statement. A lot of things get left out, and a short statement—sometimes just a word or two—is made that says a lot about a person's life. We all use life summaries. We talk about Peter, always quick to speak (but not necessarily the right things); George Washington, the father of our country; or Columbus, who discovered America. These people did many things, but we remember them for a few of the most important things they did or for the passion of their lives. There was Paul, missionary to the Gentiles, and Livingstone, missionary to Africa.

Sometimes politicians worry about how they will be remembered in history. Even though they may try to shape history by their speeches, what is remembered is more likely to come from their actions. It isn't all about talking the talk. The fact is, it is about walking the walk.

So what will people say about me? How will my obituary read? I am writing it today by the way I live. If my obituary were to be only a line or two long, what would it say?

Probably it would not say that I owned a blue car or that I got a degree from some school. I doubt if it would tell where I worked.

If I had all the options before me (and I do), then I think I would want my obituary to say, "Don Schneider was a man who was friends with Jesus. He talked, preached, and wrote about Him." Wow, that would be a wonderful and awesome obituary. I would just love it. What do you think? Would you like yours to describe your life with Jesus? I'll tell you, the only way to make it happen is to live with Him now. Just now I'm asking Jesus into my heart . . . to write on it the story of our friendship.